# DAWKINS'
# GOD

ALISTER McGRATH

# DAWKINS'
# GOD

## GENES, MEMES, AND THE
## MEANING OF LIFE

Blackwell
Publishing

© 2005 by Alister McGrath

BLACKWELL PUBLISHING
350 Main Street, Malden, MA 02148-5020, USA
108 Cowley Road, Oxford OX4 1JF, UK
550 Swanston Street, Carlton, Victoria 3053, Australia

First published 2005 by Blackwell Publishing Ltd

*Library of Congress Cataloging-in-Publication Data*

McGrath, Alister E., 1953–
    Dawkins' God : genes, memes, and the meaning of life / Alister
E. McGrath.
        p. cm.
    Includes bibliographical references and index.
    ISBN 1–4051–2539–X (hardcover: alk. paper) –
    ISBN 1–4051–2538–1 (pbk.: alk. paper)
    1. Apologetics.    2. Dawkins, Richard, 1941–    I. Title.

    BT1103.M34 2004
    261.5′5–dc22
                                                          2004010887

A catalogue record for this title is available from the British Library.

Set in 10/12.5pt Rotation
by Graphicraft Limited, Hong Kong
Printed and bound in the United Kingdom
by TJ International Ltd, Padstow, Cornwall

The publisher's policy is to use permanent paper from mills that
operate a sustainable forestry policy, and which has been
manufactured from pulp processed using acid-free and elementary
chlorine-free practices. Furthermore, the publisher ensures that the
text paper and cover board used have met acceptable environmental
accreditation standards.

For further information on
Blackwell Publishing, visit our website:
www.blackwellpublishing.com

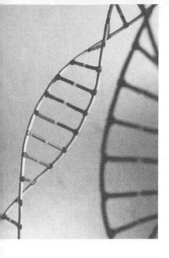

# Contents

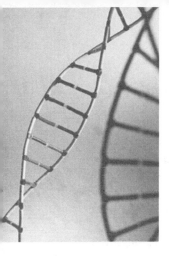

# Encountering Dawkins:
# A Personal Account

I first came across Richard Dawkins' work back in 1977, when I read his first major book, *The Selfish Gene*. I was completing my doctoral research in Oxford University's department of biochemistry, under the genial supervision of Professor Sir George Radda, who went on to become Chief Executive of the Medical Research Council. I was trying to figure out how biological membranes are able to work so successfully, by developing new physical methods of studying their behavior.

Although it would be some years before *The Selfish Gene* achieved the cult status it now enjoys, it was obviously a marvelous book. I admired Dawkins' wonderful way with words, and his ability to explain crucial – yet often difficult – scientific ideas so clearly. It was popular scientific writing at its best. No surprise, then, that the *New York Times* commented that it was "the sort of popular science writing that makes the reader feel like a genius."

It would also be some years before Dawkins' reputation as "Darwin's Rottweiler" would become established. Yet even in this early work, traces of a markedly anti-religious polemic could be discerned. While a schoolboy, I had once, like

Dawkins, believed that the natural sciences demanded an atheist worldview. But not any more. I was naturally interested to see what kind of arguments Dawkins would develop in support of this interesting idea. What I found was not particularly persuasive. He offered a few muddled attempts to make sense of the idea of "faith," without establishing a proper analytical and evidential basis for his reflections. I found myself puzzled by this, and made a mental note to pen a few words in response sometime.

I had loved the natural sciences since I can remember loving anything. When I was about ten, I built myself a small reflecting telescope so that I could study the wonders of the heavens. I found myself delighted by shimmering images of the moons of Jupiter and the craters of the moon. I was entranced by the sense of peering into a vast, awe-inspiring and mysterious universe, and not a little overwhelmed by the experience. An old German microscope, given to me by a great-uncle who was once head of pathology at the Royal Victoria Hospital, Belfast, opened up the world of biology for me (it still sits on my study desk). By the age of thirteen, I was hooked. There was no question of what I would do with the rest of my life. I would study the marvels of nature.

A change of school in 1966 injected new energy into my vision. The Methodist College, Belfast had recently constructed an entire new science block, and equipped it lavishly by the standards of the day. I threw myself into the study of the sciences and mathematics, specializing particularly in chemistry and physics. It was a labor of love, more than amply rewarded by the mental excitement it generated. At this stage, it was self-evidently true to me that the sciences had displaced God, making religious belief a rather pointless relic of a bygone age. However, my views on this were sharpened up significantly by the events of the late 1960s.

A surge of anti-religious feeling was sweeping across the face of Western culture. Tom Wolfe caught this cultural mood well in his essay "The Great Relearning": everything was to be swept aside in a frenzy of dissatisfaction, and rebuilt from ground zero.[1] Never before had such a radical Promethean reconstruction of things been possible. It was time to seize the moment, and break decisively with the past! Religion would be swept aside as the moral detritus of humanity, at best an irrelevance to real life, and at worst an evil, perverse force which enslaved humanity through its lies and delusions.

As the rhetoric of that last sentence will make quite clear, I was inclined to the worst case scenario. The natural sciences suggested that God was not required for the explanation of any aspect of the world. Yet, like many in those heady days of optimism and revolutionary fervor, I had drunk deeply at the wells of Marxism, and had come to see religion as a dangerous delusion. It was a particularly easy conclusion to reach in the midst of the religious strife of Northern Ireland at the time, and I duly drew it without much difficulty or reflection.

I now had a new reason for loving the sciences. I came across an Arab proverb that seemed to sum things up perfectly: "The enemy of my enemy is my friend." Not only were the sciences intellectually fascinating and aesthetically delightful: they also undermined the plausibility of religious belief, and hence opened the way to a better world. Religion was just an idiotic "medieval superstition" which no lover of the truth or morally serious person could tolerate. And it was on its way out. A brighter, godless tomorrow would soon be dawning. Atheism was the only option for anyone confronted with the facts. I saw my future – rather arrogantly, I fully concede – in terms of bringing light and joy through preaching the gospel of scientific atheism, and even tried (unsuccessfully) to establish an Atheist Society at my school.

I decided to study chemistry at Oxford University as a means to this end. Oxford's chemistry course was the best in the land, and I set my sights firmly on getting there. This involved staying on for an extra term at the Methodist College to receive special coaching in advanced chemistry, in preparation for the Oxford entrance examinations of December 1970. Just before Christmas, I learned that I had been offered a place at Wadham College, Oxford, to study chemistry. My cup of joy was full to overflowing.

But I was not due to go up to Oxford until October 1971. What could I do in the meantime? My schoolfriends who had also sat the scholarship examinations drifted off to travel the world or earn some serious money. I decided to stay on at school for the rest of the year, and use the time preparing for Oxford. I would learn German and Russian, both of which would be useful for reading professional chemical journals such as *Zeitschrift für physicalische Chemie* or *Zeitschrift für Naturforschung*. It would also allow me to read the works of Karl Marx, Friedrich Engels, and V. I. Lenin in their original languages. In addition, I would have time to consolidate my reading in biology, which I had neglected through concentrating so heavily on physics, chemistry, and mathematics.

After a month or so of intensive reading in the school science library, having exhausted the works on biology, I came across a section that I had never noticed before. It was labeled "The History and Philosophy of Science" and was heavy with dust. I had little time for this sort of stuff, tending to regard it as uninformed criticism of the certainties and simplicities of the natural sciences by those who felt threatened by them – what Dawkins would later call "truth-heckling."[2] Philosophy, like theology, was just pointless speculation about issues that could be solved through a few decent experiments. What was the point?

I took out a title, and began to read it. I now know that L. W. Hull's *History and Philosophy of Science: An Introduction* (1959) is a rather poor introduction to the field, noted chiefly for holding views that were fashionable way back in the Victorian period. But it got me interested, and led me on to greater things. By the time I had finished reading the somewhat meager holdings of the school library in this field, I realized that I needed to do some very serious rethinking.

Far from being half-witted obscurantism that placed unnecessary obstacles in the relentless place of scientific advance, the history and philosophy of science asked all the right questions about the reliability and limits of scientific knowledge. And they were questions that I had not faced thus far. I was like a fundamentalist Christian who suddenly discovered that Jesus had not personally written the Apostles' Creed, or a flat-earther forced to come to terms with photographs of the planet taken from space. Issues such as the underdetermination of theory by data, radical theory change in the history of science, the difficulties in devising a "crucial experiment," and the enormously complex issues associated with determining what was the "best explanation" of a given set of observations crowded in on me, muddying what I had taken to be the clear, still water of scientific truth.

Things turned out to be rather more complicated than I had realized. My eyes had been opened, and I knew there was no going back to the simplistic take on the sciences I had once known. Like many people at that stage in their education, I had enjoyed the beauty and innocence of a childlike attitude to the sciences, and secretly longed to remain in that secure place. Indeed, I think that part of me deeply wished that I had never picked up that book, never asked those awkward questions, and never questioned the simplicities of my scientific youth. But there was no going back. I had stepped through a door, and could not escape the new world I had now entered.

Studying chemistry at Oxford was an exhilarating experience, as I expected, broadening my mental horizons and creating new challenges. As things turned out, those horizons expanded in a direction I never would have anticipated. In my first term at Oxford University, late in 1971, I began to discover that Christianity was rather more interesting and considerably more exciting than I had realized. While I had been severely critical of Christianity as a young man, I had never extended that same critical evaluation to atheism, tending to assume that it was self-evidently correct, and was hence exempt from being assessed in this way. During October and November 1971, I began to discover that the intellectual case for atheism was rather less substantial than I had supposed. Far from being self-evidently true, it seemed to rest on rather shaky foundations. Christianity, on the other hand, turned out to be far more robust intellectually than I had supposed.

My doubts about the intellectual foundations of atheism began to coalesce into a realization that atheism was actually a belief system, where I had assumed it to be a factual statement about reality. I also discovered that I knew far less about Christianity than I had assumed. As I began to read Christian books and listen to Christian friends explaining what they actually believed, it gradually became clear to me that I had

5

rejected a religious stereotype. I had some major rethinking to do. By the end of November 1971, I had made my decision: I turned my back on one faith, and embraced another.

In September 1974, I joined the research group of Professor George Radda, based in Oxford University's department of biochemistry. Radda was developing a series of physical methods for investigating complex biological systems, including magnetic resonance techniques. My particular interest was developing innovative physical methods for studying the behavior of biological membranes, including the use of fluorescent probes and positron decay to investigate temperature-dependent transitions in biological systems and their models.[3]

But my real interest was shifting elsewhere. I never lost my fascination with the natural world. I just found something else rising, initially to rival it, and then to complement it. For what I had previously assumed to be the open warfare of science and religion increasingly seemed to me to represent a critical yet constructive synergy, with immense potential for intellectual enrichment. How, I found myself wondering, might the working methods and assumptions of the natural sciences be used to develop an intellectually robust Christian theology?[4] And what should I do to explore this possibility properly? I spent the summer of 1976 working at the University of Utrecht, made possible by a fellowship awarded by the European Molecular Biology Organization, and gradually came to the conclusion that I could only do this by studying for an undergraduate degree in theology, followed by advanced research in the relation of theology and science.

Happily, I had just been elected to a Senior Scholarship at Merton College, which allowed me to continue my biophysical research, while at the same time studying theology. By June 1978 I had gained my doctorate in biophysics, and an honors degree in theology, and was preparing to leave Oxford to do some theological research at Cambridge University. To my surprise, I then received an invitation to lunch with a senior editor at Oxford University Press. Oxford is a very small place, and gossip spreads very quickly. The Press had heard about my "interesting career to date," he explained, and had an interesting possibility to discuss with me. Dawkins' *Selfish Gene* had generated a huge amount of interest. Would I like to write a response from a Christian perspective?

By any standards, *The Selfish Gene* was a great read – stimulating, controversial, and informative. Dawkins had that rare ability to make complex things understandable, without talking down to his audience. Yet Dawkins did more than just make evolutionary theory intelligible. He was willing to set out its implications for every aspect of life, in effect presenting Darwinism as a universal philosophy of life, rather than a mere scientific theory. It was heady stuff – far better, in my view, than Jacques Monod's earlier work *Chance and Necessity* (1971), which explored similar themes. And, like all provocative writers, it opened up debates which were both important and intrinsically interesting – such as the existence of God, and the meaning of life. It would be a wonderful book to write. Only a fool, I remember thinking at the time, could resist such an invitation.

Well, that's me. After much thought, I wrote a polite note thanking my colleague for lunch, and explaining that I did not yet feel ready to write such a book. There were many others better qualified, in my view. It would just be a matter of time before someone else wrote a book-length response to Dawkins' ideas. So I headed off to Cambridge to do research into Christian theology, followed by ordination in the Church of England. After a period working in an English parish, I found my way back to Oxford. Although I was no longer able to undertake scientific research, Oxford University's excellent library resources meant I was able to keep up and develop my reading in the history and philosophy of science, as well as follow the most recent experimental and theoretical developments in the field.

But I had not forgotten Dawkins. His *Selfish Gene* introduced a new concept and word into the investigation of the history of ideas: the "meme." As the area of research I hoped to pursue was the history of ideas (specifically, Christian theology, but set against the backdrop of intellectual development in general), I had done a substantial amount of background research on existing models of how ideas were developed and received within and across cultures. None of them seemed satisfactory.[5] But Dawkins' theory of the "meme" – a cultural replicator – seemed to offer a brilliant new theoretical framework for exploring the general question of the origins, development, and reception of ideas, based on rigorous empirical scientific investigation. I recall with great affection a moment of sheer intellectual excitement, sometime late in 1977, when I realized that there might be a credible alternative to the stale and unpersuasive models of doctrinal development I had explored and rejected at that stage. Might this be the future?[6]

As I knew from Darwin's work on the Galapagos finches, it helps to approach the evidence with at least a provisional theoretical framework.[7] And so I began to explore using the "meme" as a model for the development of Christian doctrine. I shall report more fully on my twenty-five year evaluation of both the "meme" concept and its utility in a later chapter. Suffice it to say at this stage that I was perhaps somewhat optimistic concerning both its rigorous empirical grounding and its value as a tool for the critical study of intellectual development.

In the meanwhile, Dawkins went on to produce a series of brilliant and provocative books, each of which I devoured with interest and admiration. Dawkins followed *The Selfish Gene* with *The Extended Phenotype* (1981), *The Blind Watchmaker* (1986), *River out of Eden* (1995), *Climbing Mount Improbable* (1996), *Unweaving the Rainbow* (1998), and finally the collection of essays *A Devil's Chaplain* (2003). Yet the tone and focus of his writing changed. As philosopher Michael Ruse pointed out in a review of *The Devil's Chaplain*, Dawkins' "attention has swung from writing about science for a popular audience to waging an all-out attack on Christianity."[8] The brilliant scientific popularizer became a savage anti-religious polemicist, preaching rather than arguing (or so it seemed to me) his case.

I find fundamentalism of all kinds equally repugnant, religious or anti-religious, and was deeply distressed at this development in someone I had admired. Dawkins' account of religion tends to amount to little more than freak-pointing, with the extreme portrayed as the typical. Religious people were dismissed as anti-scientific, intellectually irresponsible, or existentially immature – on a good day.

Yet while Dawkins' atheism became more strident in its tone and more aggressive in its assertions, it did not become noticeably more sophisticated in terms of the arguments offered. Religious folk are demonized as dishonest, liars, fools, and knaves, incapable of responding honestly to the real world, and preferring to invent a false, pernicious, and delusionary world into which to entice the unwary, the young, and the naive. It is a line of thought that has led many to suggest, not entirely without reason, that Dawkins might have fallen victim to the kind of self-righteousness that biblical writers associated with the Pharisees. The writer Douglas Adams recalls Dawkins once remarking: "I really don't think I'm arrogant, but I do get impatient with people who don't share with me the same humility in front of the facts."[9] Yet the awkward fact, which Dawkins seems reluctant to concede, is that there are many sane and intelligent individuals who draw conclusions which differ completely from his through precisely that same humble engagement with the scientific evidence. Perhaps they are mad; perhaps they are bad; but then again, perhaps they are neither.

Dawkins writes with erudition and sophistication on issues of evolutionary biology, clearly having mastered the intricacies of his field and its vast research literature. Yet when he comes to deal with anything to do with God, we seem to enter into a different world. It is the world of a schoolboy debating society, relying on rather heated, enthusiastic overstatements, spiced up with some striking oversimplifications and more than an occasional misrepresentation (accidental, I can only assume) to make some superficially plausible points – the sort of arguments that once persuaded me that atheism was the only option for a thinking person when I was a schoolboy. But that was then. What about now?

Having wrestled with the implications of the scientific method for belief in God throughout my late teens, I was more than a little puzzled by the quality of the arguments offered for atheism in Dawkins' writings of the 1980s. It clearly seems self-evident to Dawkins that the natural sciences must lead to an atheist worldview on the part of any honest, intelligent person. Those who believe in God are therefore dishonest, deluded, or stupid. Yet the arguments he proposed in his published works of the late 1970s and 1980s simply did not lead to that conclusion. Dawkins' atheism seemed to be tacked onto his evolutionary biology with intellectual velcro. I had hoped that his writings would produce a new, intellectually reinvigorated atheism – something that would be really exciting and engaging. Instead, I found the same plodding rhetoric and tired old clichés that I knew well from my schoolboy days. Dawkins was preaching to the choir, recycling rather than renewing the case for atheism.

Disappointed, I duly waited for the works of the 1990s, hoping to see new and more persuasive arguments developed. Instead, I found the same stale old atheist equivalents of the "mad, bad, or God" arguments used by some Christians to prove the divinity of Christ,[10] linked rather tenuously to some interesting developments in evolutionary biology. It became increasingly clear to me that the grounds of Dawkins' atheism might ultimately lie beyond the sciences, not within them.

The year 2003 dawned, and with it came the publication of *A Devil's Chaplain*. It is not one of Dawkins' best works, not least because it consists of a collection of essentially un-related essays, often so brief as to be quite inadequate to deal properly with the questions under consideration. In any case, the book exudes intellectual weariness, as if its author had run out of intellectual steam. Yet still no book-length response to Dawkins had appeared, apart from a helpful introduction to the differences between him and Stephen Jay Gould on evolutionary issues.[11] Finally, in the summer of 2003, twenty-five years after the possibility was first mooted, I decided that it was time to pen a response.

Some might expect this book to be a religious rebuttal of Dawkins. They must look elsewhere, for it is nothing of the sort. The real issue for me is how Dawkins proceeds from a Darwinian theory of evolution to a confident atheistic world-view, which he preaches with messianic zeal and unassailable certainty.[12] As the title of the book indicates, there are some important questions to be asked about what sort of god Dawkins declares to be redundant or discredited.[13] What god is being rejected? Does this god bear any relation to rival concepts of divinity, such as the God of Christianity? And is this rejection actually warranted on the basis of the arguments Dawkins offers?

It is therefore important to appreciate from the outset that this book is not a critique of Dawkins' evolutionary biology. I do not propose to engage with Dawkins' specific views on the theory of evolution, but the broader conclusions that he draws from these, particularly concerning religion and intellectual history. His opinions on evolution must be judged by the scientific community as a whole; my concern – and the field in which I am competent to pronounce – is supremely the critically important and immensely problematic transition from *biology* to *theology*.

It is widely held that the scientific method simply cannot adjudicate on the God-question. The general view is that people tend to arrive at their religious views on other grounds, and then use their scientific ideas as retrospective validation of those views. The science is thus made to fit the worldview, and proves capable of accommodating both theist and atheist viewpoints with remarkable ease. But this received view may be wrong, and Dawkins may be the one who demonstrates that this is the case. The issues he raises are so important that they cannot be evaded, or dealt with by the sound bites or superficial pot shots that are typical of media-driven discussion. They merit full and extended discussion. What I hope to encourage is an exploration of the place of the natural sciences in shaping the world of our minds and the culture in which we live, based on Dawkins' published writings.

Dawkins holds that the explanatory force of Darwinism on the one hand, and the aesthetic, moral, and intellectual failings of religion on the other, lead the honest person directly and inexorably to atheism. Humanity has come of age. It has left its delusions behind. We can "leave the crybaby phase, and finally come of age."[14] Although I shall interact with the substance of Dawkins' religious views on occasion in this book, my interest lies primarily in why he believes them to be correct, rather than what they are in themselves. This book is a critical engagement with Dawkins' worldview, which sets out to ask whether his famously aggressive atheism is actually warranted on the basis of the arguments he presents.

Dawkins' hostility to religion is deep-rooted, and not grounded in one specific concern. Four interconnected grounds of hostility may be found throughout his writings:

1   A Darwinian worldview makes belief in God unnecessary or impossible. Although hinted at in *The Selfish Gene*, this idea is developed in detail in *The Blind Watchmaker*.
2   Religion makes assertions which are grounded in faith, which represents a retreat from a rigorous, evidence-based concern for truth. For Dawkins, truth is grounded in explicit proof; any form of obscurantism or mysticism grounded in faith is to be opposed vigorously.
3   Religion offers an impoverished and attenuated vision of the world. "The universe presented by organized religion is a poky little medieval universe, and extremely limited."[15] In contrast, science offers a bold and brilliant vision of the universe as grand, beautiful, and awe-inspiring. This aesthetic critique of religion is developed especially in his 1998 work *Unweaving the Rainbow*.
4   Religion leads to evil. It is like a malignant virus, infecting human minds. This is not strictly a scientific judgment, in that, as Dawkins often points out, the sciences cannot determine what is good or evil. "Science has no methods for deciding what is ethical."[16] It is, however, a profoundly moral objection to religion, deeply rooted within Western culture and history, which must be taken with the greatest seriousness.

So which of these is the *real* basis for Dawkins' atheism? Which are core hypotheses, and which auxiliary, to borrow the language of empiricism? In his own reflections on his intellectual development, Dawkins tends to present his atheism as arising naturally from his growing conviction of the total explanatory power of Darwinism – a development which began even during his final years at Oundle School. But what if Dawkins' atheism is actually grounded in moral considerations, and then read back into his scientific enterprise?

So why write such a book? Three reasons may be given. First, Dawkins is a fascinating writer, both in terms of the quality of the ideas he develops, and the verbal dexterity with which he defends them. Anyone who is remotely interested in ideas will find Dawkins an important sparring partner. Augustine of Hippo once wrote of the *"eros* of the mind," referring to a deep longing within the human mind to make sense of things – a passion for understanding and knowledge. Anyone sharing that passion will want to enter into the debate that Dawkins has begun.

And that thought underlies my second reason for writing this book. Yes, Dawkins seems to many to be immensely provocative and aggressive, dismissing alternative positions with indecent haste, or treating criticism of his personal views as an attack on the entire scientific enterprise. Yet this kind of overheated rhetoric is found in any popular debate, whether religious, philosophical, or scientific. Indeed, it is what makes popular debates *interesting*, and raises them above the tedious drone of normal scholarly discussion, which seems invariably to be accompanied by endless footnotes, citing of weighty but dull authorities, and cautious understatement heavily laced with qualifications. How much more exciting to have a pugnacious, no holds barred debate, without having to worry about the stifling conventions of rigorous evidence-based scholarship! Dawkins clearly wants to provoke such a debate and discussion, and it would be churlish not to accept such an invitation.

I have a third reason, however. I write as a Christian theologian who believes it is essential to listen seriously and carefully to criticism of my discipline, and respond appropriately to it. One of my reasons for taking Dawkins so seriously is that I want to ask what may be learned from him. As any serious historian of Christian thought knows, Christianity is committed to a constant review of its ideas in the light of their moorings in scripture and tradition, always asking whether any contemporary interpretation of a doctrine is adequate or acceptable. As we shall see, Dawkins offers a powerful, and in my view credible, challenge to one way of thinking about the doctrine of creation, which gained influence in England during the eighteenth century, and lingers on in some quarters today. He is a critic who needs to be heard, and taken seriously.

But enough of such preliminaries. Let's get on with it, and start delving into the Darwinian worldview which Dawkins has done so much to explore and commend.

Alister McGrath
Oxford

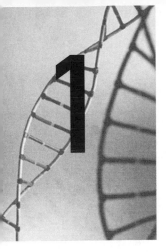

# The Selfish Gene: A Darwinian View of the World

Why are things the way they are? And what does this tell us about the meaning of life? These two questions, naive yet profound, have played a decisive role in shaping Western thinking about the world. From the beginning of human civilization, people have wondered what explanation might be offered for the structures of the world – like the stars in the night sky, natural wonders such as a rainbow, and the mysterious behavior of living beings. Not only do these wonders evoke a sense of awe; they also call out for explanation.

The earliest Greek philosophers – the "pre-Socratics" – argued endlessly about the nature of the world, and how it came to be as it is. They insisted that the universe was rationally constructed, and that it could therefore be understood through the right use of human reason and argument. Human beings had the ability to make sense of the universe. Socrates took this line of thought further, identifying a link between the way the universe was constructed and the best way for human beings to live. To reflect on the nature of the universe was to gain insights into the nature of the "good life" – the best and most authentic way of living. Reflecting on the clues provided in the structuring of the world thus leads to an understanding of our identity and destiny.

For many, the answer lay in the divine origins of the world – the idea that, in some way, the world has been ordered or constructed. Many have found this idea to be spiritually attractive and intellectually satisfying. Isaac Newton comes to mind. So does John Polkinghorne, who famously resigned the Chair of Mathematical Physics at Cambridge University in 1979 in order to study Christian theology. For Richard Dawkins, however, the advent of Charles Darwin has shown this up as "cosmic sentimentality," "saccharine false purpose," which natural science has a moral mission to purge and debunk. Such naive beliefs, he argues, might have been understandable before Darwin came along. But not now. Darwin has changed everything. Newton would be an atheist if he had been born after Darwin. Before Darwin, atheism was just one among many religious possibilities; now, it is the only serious option for a thinking, honest, and scientifically-informed person. To believe in God nowadays is to be "hoodwink'd with faery fancy."

Once upon a time such religious beliefs would have been understandable, perhaps even forgivable. But not now. Humanity was once an infant. Now, we have grown up, and discarded infantile explanations. And Darwin is the one who marks that decisive point of transition. Intellectual history is thus divided into two epochs: before Darwin, and after Darwin. As James Watson, the Nobel Prize winner and co-discoverer of the structure of DNA put it, "Charles Darwin will eventually be seen as a far more influential figure in the history of human thought than either Jesus Christ or Mohammed."

But why Darwin? Why not Karl Marx? Or Sigmund Freud? Each of these is regularly proposed as having brought about an intellectual earthquake, shattering prevailing assumptions and ushering in radical new ways of thinking which lead to the bifurcation of human thought. The theories of biological evolution, historical materialism, and psychoanalysis have all been proposed as defining the contours of humanity come of age. All, interestingly, have been linked with atheism, the movement that the nineteenth and early twentieth centuries hoped would prove to be an intellectual and political liberator. So why Darwin?

To ask this question is to open up the issues which so deeply concern Dawkins, and which have such wider implications.

## Introducing Dawkins

But first, let us introduce Dawkins. Clinton Richard Dawkins was born in Kenya on March 26, 1941, the son of Clinton John and Jean Mary Vyvyan Dawkins. His religious background, he tells us, was traditional Anglicanism, although there are hints that he was intrigued in his youth by the ideas of the French Jesuit paleontologist Pierre Teilhard de Chardin concerning the relation of evolution and spirituality.[1]

After attending Oundle School, he went up to Balliol College, Oxford, to read zoology, in 1959. After graduating in 1962, he went on to undertake research in Oxford University's department of zoology under the supervision of Professor Niko Tinbergen (1907–88), joint winner of the Nobel Prize in Medicine and Physiology for 1973.

Tinbergen and his Austrian colleague Konrad Lorenz (1903–89) pioneered ethology – the study of whole patterns of animal behavior in natural environments, stressing the analysis of adaptation and the evolution of patterns. Although Lorenz may be argued to have laid the conceptual foundations for the discipline in the 1930s, Tinbergen's patient and detailed observational work is widely credited with its later conceptual and practical development, especially through his landmark work *The Study of Instinct* (1951).[2] Dawkins' doctoral thesis, entitled "Selective Pecking in the Domestic Chick," stands firmly within this tradition. Its subject was tight and well defined: what mechanism may be proposed to account for the way in which a chick pecks at the stimuli around it?

Dawkins relates how his research was inspired by a lecture he had heard from Professor N. S. Sutherland (1927–98), who left Oxford in 1964 to found the Laboratory of Experimental Psychology at the recently established University of Sussex. His work focused on developing a "Threshold Model" which might account for a detailed series of experimental observations concerning the timing and orientation of chick pecks at

Plate 1    Richard Dawkins (born 1941) © Rex Features

small hemispherical spots, presented in pairs. His data was processed using an Eliot 803 machine – an early computer, which relied on punched tape for its data. The thesis was submitted in June 1966, and accepted later that year.

Dawkins then spent a year doing postdoctoral research, along with some lecturing in the department of zoology. Tinbergen was on sabbatical leave during the academic year 1966–7, and asked Dawkins to cover some of his lectures, while at the same time writing up his thesis for publication.[3] Dawkins' lectures allowed him to explore some aspects of W. D. Hamilton's theory of kin selection, including the question of how certain apparently cooperative forms of behavior arise.[4] An individual behaves in such a way that the reproductive capacity of another individual is enhanced, even to the detriment of its own selective capacity. The phenomenon may be observed in aspects of the social, parental, and mating behavior of animals. So how could this have evolved?

Dawkins came to the conclusion that the "most imaginative way of looking at evolution, and the most inspiring way of teaching it," was to see the entire process from the perspective of the gene. The genes, for their own good, are "manipulating" and directing the bodies that contain them and carry them about. Throughout his writings, Dawkins has developed the rhetoric of a gene's eye view of things – not simply of the individual, but of the entire living world. Organisms can be reduced to genes, and genes to digital (not analogue) information.

Life is just bytes and bytes of bytes of digital information. Genes are pure information – information that can be encoded, recoded and decoded, without any degradation or change of meaning . . . We – and that means all living things – are survival machines programmed to propagate the digital database that did the programming. Darwinism is now seen to be the survival of the survivors at the level of pure, digital, code.[5]

In effect, Dawkins was arguing that we should extrapolate from Hamilton's theory of kin selection, and apply it to every aspect of social behavior. Animals were to be seen as "machines carrying their instructions around" with them, using their every aspect as "levers of power to propel the genes into the next generation." Because kin groups share the same genes, the sacrifice of an individual may still increase the likelihood of those genes surviving within the gene group as a whole. Dawkins can be regarded as the first, and still the most systematic, ethologist of the gene. It is this central theme which has been so decisive to his way of seeing the world, and we shall explore it in much greater detail presently.

From Oxford, Dawkins went on to become Assistant Professor of Zoology at the University of California at Berkeley in 1967, returning to Oxford as Lecturer in Zoology and Fellow of New College in 1970. It was during this time that his most influential and creative works were published, including *The Selfish Gene* and *The Blind Watchmaker*. In 1995 he was appointed to a new academic position at Oxford University, made possible by the generosity of Charles Simonyi, then one of the Microsoft Corporation's foremost software architects, who went on to co-found the Intentional Software Corporation in August 2002. Dawkins was appointed as the first "Charles Simonyi Reader in the Public Understanding of Science."

A further advance in his career took place in 1996, when Oxford University conferred on Dawkins the additional title of "Professor of the Public Understanding of Science," thus saddling Dawkins with the eminent, yet somewhat cumbersome, distinction of being both "Charles Simonyi Reader in the Public Understanding of Science" and "Professor of the Public Understanding of Science." Oxford University recommends that he be styled in a somewhat more simplified manner, as "Simonyi Reader, and Professor of the Public Understanding of Science."[6] He was made a Fellow of the Royal Society – the supreme accolade for a British scientist – in May 2001.

So where shall we begin to explore the ideas that give Dawkins such animation? Perhaps the best place is with Charles Darwin himself, who laid the foundations for Dawkins' approach, and the worldview he constructed as a result.

## The New Approach: Charles Darwin

The publication of Charles Darwin's *Origin of Species* (1859) is rightly regarded as a landmark in nineteenth-century science. On December 27, 1831, HMS *Beagle* set out from the southern English port of Plymouth on a voyage that lasted almost five years. Its mission was to complete a survey of the southern coasts of South America, and afterwards to circumnavigate the globe. The small ship's naturalist was Charles Darwin (1809–82). During the voyage, Darwin noted some aspects of the plant and animal life of South America, particularly the Galapagos Islands and Tierra del Fuego, which seemed to him to require explanation, yet which were not satisfactorily accounted for by existing theories. The opening words of *Origin of Species* set out the riddle that he was determined to solve:

When on board HMS *Beagle* as naturalist, I was much struck with certain facts in the distribution of the organic beings inhabiting South America, and in the geological relations of the present to the past inhabitants of that continent. These facts, as will be seen in the latter chapters of this volume, seemed to throw some light on the origin of species – that mystery of mysteries, as it has been called by one of our greatest philosophers.

One popular account of the origin of species, widely supported by the religious and academic establishment of the early nineteenth century, held that God had somehow created everything more or less as we now see it. The success of the view owed much to the influence of William Paley (1743–1805), archdeacon of Carlisle, who compared God to one of the mechanical geniuses of the Industrial Revolution. God had directly created the world in all its intricacy. We shall explore the origins and influence of Paley's thinking in the next chapter; at this stage, we need merely note that Paley was of the view that God had constructed – Paley prefers the word "contrived" – the world in its finished form, as we now know it. The idea of any kind of development seemed impossible to him. Did a watchmaker leave his work unfinished? Certainly not!

Darwin knew of Paley's views, and initially found them persuasive. However, his observations on the *Beagle* raised some questions. On his return, Darwin set out to develop a more satisfying explanation of his own observations and those of others. Although Darwin appears to have hit on the basic idea of evolution through natural selection by 1842, he was not ready to publish. Such a radical theory would require massive observational evidence to be marshaled in its support.

Some earlier works advocating the evolution of species – most notably, Robert Chambers' *Vestiges of the Natural History of Creation* (1844) – were so incompetent scientifically that they threatened to discredit the ideas that they tried to advance.[7] Thomas H. Huxley, who would later champion Darwin's theory, damned the book as a "once attractive and still notorious work of fiction," and its author as one of "those who . . . indulge in science at second-hand and dispense totally with logic." Chambers was a publisher, not a scientist, and was a little naive at points – for example, in taking seriously a highly improbable report that living creatures had resulted from passing electric currents through potassium ferrocyanate solution.

As a result of Chambers' muddying of the waters, there was now no way that a radical new theory of biological origins could be launched without overwhelming documentation, guaranteed to disarm its critics through its sheer weight of data. Darwin's *Origin of Species* would offer the world both evidence of biological evolution, and an explanation of its mechanism. On his return to England, Darwin set about building up his repository of evidence.

Four features of the natural world seemed to Darwin to require particularly close attention, in the light of problems and shortcomings with existing explanations.

1  The forms of certain living creatures seemed to be adapted to their specific needs. Paley's theory proposed that these creatures were individually designed by God with those needs in mind. Darwin increasingly regarded this as a clumsy explanation.

2  Some species were known to have died out altogether – to have become extinct. This fact had been known before Darwin, and was often explained on the basis of "catastrophe" theories, such as a "universal flood," as suggested by the biblical account of Noah.

3  Darwin's research voyage on the *Beagle* had persuaded him of the uneven geographical distribution of life forms throughout the world. In particular, Darwin was impressed by the peculiarities of island populations.

4  Many creatures possess "rudimentary structures," which have no apparent or predictable function – such as the nipples of male mammals, the rudiments of a pelvis and

hind limbs in snakes, and wings on many flightless birds. How might these be explained on the basis of Paley's theory, which stressed the importance of the individual design of species? Why should God design redundancies?

These aspects of the natural order could all be accounted for by Paley's theory. Yet the explanations offered seemed unduly cumbersome and strained. What was originally a relatively neat and elegant theory began to crumble under the weight of accumulated difficulties and tensions. There had to be a better explanation. Darwin offered a wealth of evidence in support of the idea of biological evolution, and proposed a mechanism by which it might work: *natural selection*.

The *Origin of Species* sets out with great care why the idea of "natural selection" is the best mechanism to explain how the evolution of species took place, and how it is to be understood. The key point is that natural selection is proposed as nature's analogue to the process of "artificial selection" in stockbreeding. Darwin was familiar with these issues, especially as they related to the breeding of pigeons.[8] The first chapter of the *Origin of Species* therefore considers "variation under domestication" – that is, the way in which domestic plants and animals are bred by agriculturists. Darwin notes how selective breeding allows farmers to create animals or plants with particularly desirable traits. Variations develop in successive generations through this process of breeding, and these can be exploited to bring about inherited characteristics which are regarded as being of particular value by the breeder. In the second chapter, Darwin introduces the key notions of the "struggle for survival" and "natural selection" to account for what may be observed in both the fossil records and the present natural world.

Darwin then argues that this process of "domestic selection" or "artificial selection" offers a model for a mechanism for what happens in nature. "Variation under domestication" is presented as an analogue of "variation under nature." A process of "natural selection" is argued to occur within the natural order which is analogous to a well-known process, familiar to English stockbreeders and horticulturists: "As man can

Plate 2    Charles Darwin (1809–82) © Bettmann/CORBIS

produce and certainly has produced a great result by his
methodical and unconscious means of selection, what may not
nature effect?"

Darwin's theory had considerable explanatory force – a point
recognized by many at the time, even those who were anxious
about the implications of his ideas for the place of humanity

within nature. Yet there was a serious problem with the theory. How did nature "remember" and "transmit" these new developments? How could a rising generation "inherit" the traits of its predecessor? What mechanism could be proposed by which these new developments could be passed on to future generations? Darwin's contemporaries generally believed that characteristics of the parents were "blended" when they were passed to the offspring. But if this was the case, how could a single mutation be spread throughout a species? It would be diluted to the point of insignificance, like a drop of ink in a bucket of water. It seemed that Darwin's evolutionary hypothesis was in genetic difficulties. Variation would simply become diluted. A new trait would be like a teaspoon of white paint falling into a vat of black treacle: it would vanish from sight.

Darwin was fully aware of the need for a comprehensive account of the mechanics of inheritance. The theory he developed (known as "pangenesis") was based on hypothetical "gemmules" – minute particles which somehow determine all characteristics of the organism.[9] These "gemmules" had never been observed; nevertheless, Darwin argued that it was necessary to propose their existence to make sense of the observational data at his disposal. Each and every cell of an organism, and even parts of cells, was understood to produce gemmules of a specific type corresponding to the cell or cell part. These are able to circulate throughout the body and enter the reproductive system. Every sperm and egg contains these hypothetical gemmules, and are thus transmitted to the next generation. It was an ingenious solution; yet it was not right.[10] Darwin's theory faltered, lacking a plausible theory of genetics.

## The Mechanics of Inheritance: Mendel and Genetics

Unknown to Darwin, the issues that he was finding so troublesome were being investigated at that time in a quiet monastery garden in central Europe. Gregor Mendel (1822–84) was a monk who entered the Augustinian monastery of St. Thomas in the Austrian town of Brünn (now the Czech town of Brno) during his twenties. His monastic superiors were impressed

Plate 3    Gregor Mendel (1822–84) © Science Photo Library

with his enthusiasm but not his existing levels of education. They sent him to the University of Vienna for further study (1851–3), during which time he specialized in physics, chemistry, zoology, and botany. After returning to the monastery, he taught in a local school, and conducted some experiments in the monastery garden. He had been encouraged by both his teachers at the University of Vienna and the Abbot of his monastery to explore his interest in hybridization in plant populations. In effect, Mendel studied the heredity of specific characteristics as they were passed on from parent plants to their offspring. These experiments came to an end when he was elected Abbot of the monastery in 1868, and faced new administrative responsibilities.

Mendel's experiments involved growing something like 28,000 pea plants over the period 1856–63 and observing how characteristics were transmitted from one generation to the next. He chose to focus on seven easily determined characteristics of his peas. Two of the best known of these are the color of their flowers (purple or white?) and the color of their seeds (yellow or green?). As he observed the patterns of inheritance of these characteristics, Mendel noticed some significant recurring features. Because he used so many plants and recorded his findings so meticulously, his results could be subjected to detailed statistical analysis which disclosed certain regular, recurring mathematical patterns of immense importance. In cross-pollinating plants that either produce yellow or green peas exclusively, Mendel found that the first offspring generation always has yellow peas. However, the following generation consistently has a 3:1 ratio of yellow to green. Certain characteristics, such as yellow seeds, were found to be "dominant" over other "recessive" characteristics, such as green seeds.

From his research, Mendel was able to formulate three fundamental principles which seemed to govern inheritance:

1 The inheritance of each trait – such as the color of the flower or seed – seems to be determined by certain units or factors that are passed on to descendants.
2 An individual plant inherits one such unit from each parent for each of these traits.
3 Traits which do not show up in an individual may nevertheless be passed on to a later generation.

Mendel thus proposed a theory of "particulate inheritance," in which characteristics were determined by discrete units of inheritance that were passed intact from one generation to the next. Adaptive mutations could spread slowly through a species and never be "blended out," as some contemporary theories of genetics held. The evolutionary implications of this were considerable. Darwin's theory of natural selection, building on small mutations over long periods of time, suddenly became much more plausible.

Mendel set out his ideas at the Natural History Society of Brno early in 1865. They were received politely, but not enthusiastically, and were published the following year.[11]

Conventional accounts of this affair hold that hardly anyone read the *Verhandlungen des naturforschenden Vereins in Brünn*, and the article languished unnoticed, despite having been sent to the libraries of some 120 institutions, including the Royal Society and the Linnean Society in London. Mendel mailed an additional forty reprints of the article to prominent botanists, but they seem to have attracted little attention. It was only in 1900 that Mendel's Laws were rediscovered by Carl Correns in Germany, Hugo de Vries in the Netherlands, and Erich von Tschermak-Seysenegg in Austria, and their significance appreciated.[12]

Yet contemporary German-language sources suggest that Mendel's views were relatively well known at this time,[13] being cited in such widely distributed works as the *Catalogue of Scientific Papers of the Royal Society* (1879), Focke's *Die Pflanzen-Mischlinge* (1881), and the *Encyclopaedia Britannica* (1881). There is another explanation for why Mendel's views were ignored – namely, that they were seen to be in tension with Darwin's ideas, which were rapidly becoming accepted as scientific orthodoxy. Indeed, such was the hostility towards Mendel within some circles that some even questioned the reliability of his experiments. Mendel, it was argued, would have opposed Darwin's theory of evolution. Could his results be trusted, given this personal agenda?[14]

There were also some other reasons for expressing caution about Mendel's work. In 1930 the British mathematical biologist Ronald A. Fisher published a landmark work in Darwinian theory, which argued that Mendel's empirical results could have been predicted by an armchair scientist, armed only with "a few very simple assumptions" concerning the Mendelian notion of "factorial inheritance."[15] Fisher also suggested, on mathematical grounds, that Mendel's reported observations were just too good to be true. Mendel's segregation ratios were far higher than the principles of variation statistics would permit. Since such segregation ratios could occur only very seldom, the integrity of Mendel's ideas would have to be reconsidered. This view is still encountered. As recently as 1991, it was argued that Mendel's "account of his experiments is neither truthful nor scientifically likely," and that "most of the experiments described in *Versuche* are to be considered fictitious."[16] However, the basis of such criticisms is generally regarded as discredited, and there seems to be no real case to answer.[17]

What is particularly interesting, however, is that Mendel possessed a copy of Darwin's *Origin of Species*,[18] and marked the following passage with double lines in the margin. It was clearly of considerable importance to him. In Darwin's original English, this reads:

The slight degree of variability in hybrids from the first cross or in the first generation, in contrast with their extreme variability in the succeeding generations, is a curious fact and deserves attention.[19]

As Mendel's most distinguished biographer pointed out, this curiosity would not remain mysterious for much longer: "Mendel must have felt some gratification in the thought that his theory was soon to explain this curious fact."[20] Mendel seems to have appreciated the importance of his own ideas to Darwin. Yet Darwin, as far as can be seen, never knew of Mendel's ideas, nor their far-reaching implications for his own theory.

Dawkins himself points out that things would have been very different if Darwin had had access to these results.[21] He suggests that "Mendel perhaps did not realize the significance of his findings, otherwise he might have written to Darwin."[22] I am inclined to suspect that he did, as the unusually heavy marking of that passage from the *Origin of Species* indicates, but felt that he had already done enough to publicize his results. After all, he was a monk, and hence perhaps disinclined to any further self-advertisement. In any case, his treatise was listed in several major British English-language sources by 1881.

Mendel had shown that inheritance seemed to be determined by certain "units" or "factors." But what were they? This brings us to the discovery of the gene, an important event in its own right, and of fundamental importance to Dawkins' exposition of a Darwinian worldview.

## The Discovery of the Gene

The significance of Mendel's ideas had been appreciated in the English-speaking world by William Bateson, who expended considerable effort in attempting to clarify the principles governing inherited characteristics or traits. By 1905 it was clear that certain traits were linked in some manner, although the pattern of coupling (later to be interpreted as "complete" and "incomplete" coupling) was far from clear. Bateson used a series of vague physical analogies – such as "coupling" and "repulsion" – in an ultimately unsuccessful attempt to explain his puzzling observations. It is clear from Bateson's writings that he appears to have thought in terms of certain forces (analogous to magnetic or electrical forces) which were capable of attracting or repelling factors of genetic significance. In the end, the solution was set out in a seminal paper published by Thomas Hunt Morgan in 1926. The solution? The gene.

Excited by Mendel's ideas, Morgan had exploited the short reproductive cycle of the fruit fly *Drosophila melanogaster* to explore the transmission of heritable characteristics. Like Mendel, he chose to focus on some well-defined characteristic traits that occurred in pairs. The most famous of these was the color of the eyes. Noting the patterns of distribution of red and white eyes, Morgan modified Mendel's theory in an important respect: he argued that not all genetic traits are passed on independently, as Mendel had supposed. Instead, some genetic traits seemed to be linked, and are thus inherited together, rather than individually.

Morgan's most important conclusion concerned the "units" or "factors" which transmitted these traits, now known as "genes." It had been known for some time that the division of cells was accompanied by the appearance of tiny rod-shaped, threadlike structures, known as "chromosomes." Some had speculated that these chromosomes might be responsible for transmitting hereditary information. Morgan was able to provide overwhelming evidence that this was indeed the case. The "genes" responsible for transmitting this information were physically located on the chromosomes. As microscopes with increasing resolution were developed, it eventually became possible to confirm this visually.

Morgan's fruit flies had four unusually large chromosomes, which made them particularly easy to study microscopically. He discovered that there were four distinct groups of traits that appeared to be inherited together, corresponding exactly with the number of pairs of chromosomes observed in *Drosophila*. He also found that one of the four linkage groups had fewer characteristics than the other three. This seemed to tie in with the fact that one of the *Drosophila* chromosomes was smaller than the other three. While further work on the role in hereditary transmission of the chromosomes in the cell nucleus was still needed, a coherent picture was now beginning to emerge.

The principles of hereditary transmission was now known to be based on the Mendelian notion of discrete hereditary factors ("genes"). What is known as the "neo-Darwinism" synthesis was now possible – Mendelian genetics as the basic explanation of evolutionary change, linked with the process of Darwinian natural selection as determining its outcome. Yet further clarification was needed concerning the molecular basis of genetics. A decisive step forward was made in the United States during World War II – to which we now turn.

## The Role of DNA in Genetics

Morgan's discovery of the critical role of the chromosomes in genetics sparked off new interest in their chemical composition. What were these threadlike fibers actually made of? The Swiss biochemist Friedrich Miescher (1844–95) established the chemical composition of cell nuclei in 1868. He determined that they contained two basic components: a nucleic acid (now known as deoxyribonucleic acid, and universally known by its acronym DNA) and a class of proteins (now known as histones). These nucleic acids were not regarded as particularly important biologically. Chemical studies suggested they were not very diverse and they had only a small number of components.

31

In 1938, Phoebus Levene (1869–1940), working at the Rockefeller Institute in New York, discovered that DNA existed as a remarkably long polymer. However, he took the view that this long polymer simply consisted of repeated units of four basic nucleotides: adenine (A), guanine (G), thymine (T), and cytosine (C). For this reason, many (including Levene himself) regarded DNA as highly unlikely to have any major role in the transmission of inherited characteristics. It was too simple chemically to encode genetic information. Many believed that the ultimate key to the molecular basis of genetics would lie in proteins found within the chromosomes.

DNA deoxyribonucleic acid, the molecule that contains the genetic code. It consists of two long, twisted chains (a "double helix") made up of nucleotides. Each nucleotide contains one base, one phosphate molecule, and the sugar deoxyribose. The bases in DNA nucleotides are adenine, thymine, guanine, and cytosine.

RNA ribonucleic acid, the molecule that carries out DNA's instructions for making proteins. It consists of one long chain made up of nucleotides. Each nucleotide contains one base, one phosphate molecule, and the sugar ribose. The bases in RNA nucleotides are adenine, uracil, guanine, and cytosine. There are three main types of RNA: messenger RNA, transfer RNA, and ribosomal RNA.

As is so often the case, the key to solving this riddle came from an unexpected source. In 1928 an English medical worker, Fred Griffith, was involved in investigating a pneumonia epidemic in London. While investigating the *pneumococcus* responsible for this outbreak, Griffith made the surprising discovery that live *pneumococci* could acquire genetic traits from other, dead *pneumococci* in a process he termed "transformation." But how could this be? All that the dead *pneumococci* could transmit were chemicals: specifically, two types of nucleic acid – ribonucleic acid (RNA) and deoxyribonucleic acid (DNA) – and protein. How could these bring about genetic change in living cells?

The importance of Griffith's work was not appreciated until a research team headed by Oswald Avery replicated his findings at the Rockefeller Institute in New York. Avery and his team began detailed studies of how genetic information was transmitted to living *pneumococci*. They conducted a series of experiments which demonstrated that genetic information was not mediated by proteins, or by RNA, but specifically by DNA.[23] This was a momentous discovery, even if it would be some time before its full implications were appreciated. If DNA – and no other substance – was the carrier of hereditary information, it must have a much more complex structure than had previously been appreciated. Yet nobody knew what this structure was, nor how DNA was able to play such a critical genetic role.

This gave new impetus to a remarkable series of studies. Rosalind Franklin (1920–58) undertook pioneering X-ray crystallography work on DNA, which did much to facilitate the groundbreaking work of the English physicist Francis Crick (b. 1916) and the American geneticist James Watson (b. 1928) demonstrating a double helix structure for DNA.[24] This achievement was a remarkable physical discovery in itself. Yet it also opened the way to understanding how DNA could pass on genetic information. Watson and Crick immediately realized that the pairing of the bases in this double-stranded DNA had to be the key to its function as a replicator and as the transmitter of genetic information. They wrote: "It has not escaped our notice that the specific pairing we have postulated immediately suggests a possible copying mechanism for the genetic material." In other words, a knowledge of the physical structure of DNA suggested a mechanism by which it could replicate itself.

On the basis of this research, Crick proposed what he called the "Central Dogma" – namely, that DNA replicates, acting as a template for RNA, which in turn acts as a template for proteins. The long and complex DNA molecule contains the genetic information necessary for transmission "encoded" using the four basic nucleotides: adenine (A), guanine (G), thymine (T), and cytosine (C) arranged in sequences of "base pairs" (in that adenine is always linked to thymine, and guanine to cytosine in the double helix structure of DNA), attached to a sugar and phosphate spine. It is the sequence of these base pairs which determines the genetic information transmitted.[25]

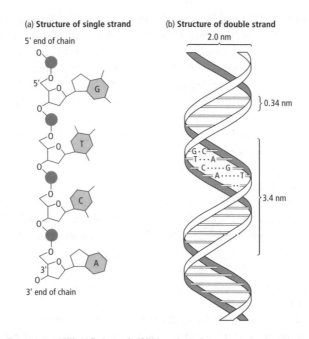

**Plate 4** The structure of DNA: (a) Each strand of DNA is made up of a sequence of nucleotide units, consisting of a base, a phosphate molecule, and the sugar deoxyribose. The bases in DNA nucleotides are adenine (A), thymine (T), guanine (G), and cytosine (C). (b) The full DNA molecule has two complementary strands, arranged in a double helix. The width of the helix is typically 2 nanometers — in other words, two billionths of a meter.

Source: Ridley, Mark. *Evolution, Third Edition.* Oxford: Blackwell Publishing, 2004, p. 23. Reprinted with permission.

So why is this so important for an understanding of evolutionary biology? The most important point to emphasize is that Darwin's theory of natural selection required variation to take place *and* to be transmitted, rather than diluted, to following generations. Natural selection would then take place, determining whether or not the genetic code for this variation would survive. The neo-Darwinian synthesis is grounded in the assumption that small random genetic changes (mutations) over long periods of time occasionally have positive survival value. Organisms possessing these favorable mutations should have relative advantage in survival and reproduction, and they will tend to pass their characteristics on to their descendants. Assuming that there are differential rates of survival, it is not

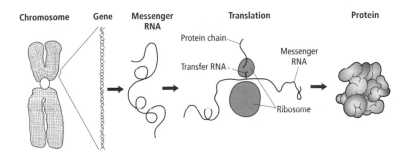

Plate 5   The transfer of information in a cell

Source: Ridley, Mark. *Evolution, Third Edition.* Oxford: Blackwell Publishing, 2004, p. 27. Reprinted with permission.

difficult to see how a favorable characteristic can become established and transmitted.

The key point is that genetic variation takes place in nature, that the process of natural selection determines whether this variation survives, and that the process of genetic replication ensures that this variation is transmitted. This, however, still leaves open many of the problems of evolutionary biology. To give an example: at what level does natural selection take place? Is it at the level of genes themselves? Or of individual organisms which contain those genes? Or at the level of kin (closely related individuals) or groups?

At this point, we have laid the foundations for a proper engagement with Richard Dawkins' views on the "selfish gene," and may now turn to explore them in much greater detail.

## Dawkins' Approach: The Selfish Gene

For Dawkins, the most satisfying rationale of the evolutionary process is framed in terms of gene lineages. The changes required for evolution to develop take place very slowly. The life of an individual organism, or a group of organisms, is small in comparison with the time required for these changes to come about. This demands a stable and very long-term unit of genetic transmission – and only gene lineages can satisfy this condition. As Richard Alexander pointed out, "genes are the most persistent of all living units, hence on all counts the most likely units of selection."[26] For Dawkins, evolution is therefore the struggle of gene lineages to replicate.

[The gene] does not grow senile; it is no more likely to die when it is a million years old than when it is only a hundred. It leaps from body to body down the generations, manipulating body after body in its own way and for its own ends, abandoning a succession of mortal bodies before they sink in senility and death. The genes are the immortals, or rather, they are defined as genetic entities that come close to deserving the title.[27]

While individual DNA molecules might survive for little more than months, their ability to replicate themselves means that any given DNA molecule "could theoretically live on in the form of *copies* of itself for a hundred million years."[28] In contrast, the individual organisms or groups of organisms are short-lived, and do not extend over the time-scales necessary to perpetuate the changes that slowly accumulate over extended lengths of time. "Genetically speaking, individuals and groups are like clouds in the sky or dust-storms in the desert. They are temporary aggregations or federations. They are not stable through evolutionary time."[29] Everything, therefore, depends on the gene.

So how do genetic changes come about? Is there not, on the face of it, an obvious and fatal contradiction between Dawkins' emphasis upon the "high copying fidelity" of replicators and the appearance of change? If replicators transmit digital information so accurately, how can change come about? Surely the fidelity of transmission points to a static, not dynamic, situation?

It is an important question, which seems to raise formidable difficulties. Certain species do indeed seem to have undergone relatively little development over huge periods of time – for example, oysters and the ginkgo tree seem to have changed relatively little over the last 150 million years.[30] Yet changes do occur. How? The theory of this had been more or less sorted out before Dawkins penned *The Selfish Gene*. In his *Chance and Necessity* (1971), the French Nobel Laureate Jacques Monod set out the basic consensus then emerging within molecular biology. Monod pointed out that genetic mutations can be observed in the laboratory. Rare, spontaneous mutations are observed in populations of *Drosophila* or other model organisms; others can be induced at random through using mutagens, such as certain chemicals or radiation. Why should not such mutations also arise over time in nature itself?

In nature itself, mutations are believed to arise accidentally, unpredictably, and for a variety of reasons. But once these changes are "incorporated in the DNA structure, the accident – essentially unpredictable because always singular – will be mechanically and faithfully replicated and translated."[31] The outcomes of these genetic mutations are then passed on within the evolutionary process, which acts as a "filter," determining whether they and their genetic codes survive. Most do not. "The replicative system, far from being able to eliminate the microscopic perturbations by which it is inevitably beset, knows only how to register and offer them – almost always in vain – to the teleonomic filter by which their performance is finally judged through natural selection."[32]

Dawkins does not endorse Monod's emphasis on the decisive role of "blind chance." While recognizing that many had indeed drawn the conclusion that Darwinism was a "theory of chance," Dawkins insisted that this was a misrepresentation of the situation. "Chance is a minor ingredient in the Darwinian recipe, but the most important ingredient is cumulative selection which is quintessentially *non*-random."[33] Evolution can thus be seen as the outcome of the non-random survival of randomly varying replicators, with the emphasis placed upon the regularity of selection rather than the happenstance of variation. Random changes in DNA give rise to new organisms, which reproduce and are subject to the pressure of natural selection. "Core Darwinism" could thus be defined as the "minimal theory that evolution is guided in adaptively non-random directions by the non-random survival of small random hereditary changes."[34]

So what about individual organisms, or groups? Although a hasty reading of Dawkins might suggest that evolution is conceived in purely molecular terms, involving only a silent and invisible competition between genes, it soon becomes clear that he avoids any such absurdity. In that organisms are the "vehicle" by which genes are passed on, the capacity of the organism to survive and reproduce becomes of immense importance. The process of selection is not competition between genes *per se* (how could that happen?), but takes places at the level of intermediaries: namely, the "vehicles" which bear or embody those genes.

A monkey is a machine that preserves genes up trees, a fish is a machine that preserves genes in the water; there is even a small worm that preserves genes in German beer mats.[35]

These "gene survival machines" reproduce their genes, and die; it is the *genes* that survive, not the vehicles, in the form of information copies of themselves. As Dawkins points out, bodies therefore tend to "have what it takes to propagate genes" and may properly be regarded as "engines of gene propagation." This distinction could be formalized in terms of the *replicators* and *vehicles* – that is, between small genetic units ("genes") themselves, and the higher level entities (typically organisms, but sometimes a family of genetically related organisms) which transmit those genes onward in the evolutionary process.[36]

In *The Selfish Gene* Dawkins offered what might be called an "ethology of the gene" – although genes cannot really be said to "behave" or "act" – which shifted the emphasis away from individual animals, or groups of animals, as the unit of evolution to the nature of the genes themselves. This "gene's eye view of the world" regards an individual organism as a "survival machine," a "passive receptacle for genes," or a "colony of genes." Dawkins stresses that this is not to suggest that such organisms have no individuality of their own; his point is that these individual characteristics are genetically determined, and hence contribute to whether that lineage of genes will be successful or not. We must "deeply imbibe the fundamental truth that an organism is a tool of DNA rather than the other way round."[37] Evolution thus occurs when genetically caused traits are passed on to the next generation.

So what is a gene? Here, we encounter a number of widely acknowledged difficulties. The term is capable of being defined or visualized in quite different ways. In a classic paper, Seymour Benzer offered an essentially molecular definition of the concept,[38] which attempted to bridge the gap between the classic view of the gene as an indivisible unit of genetic information, and the newly discovered physical structure of DNA, which showed that the molecular basis of genetics consisted of a sequence of nucleotides. Dawkins is fully aware of this meaning of the term, but points out that it is perfectly acceptable to conceptualize the "gene" in terms of the unit involved in creating a Darwinian adaptation. His definition, borrowed from George C. Williams, is as follows: "any portion of chromosomal material that potentially lasts for enough generations to serve as a unit of natural selection."[39] It is a functional definition, but is perfectly acceptable, despite the grumblings of population geneticists. However, it does lead to a troubling degree of circularity, in that it makes it almost true by definition that the gene is the unit of selection.

Williams himself wasn't entirely happy about this definition.[40] Dawkins, he argued, defined a replicator in such a way that it had to be conceived "as a physical entity duplicating itself in a reproductive process." While not necessarily disagreeing with this, Williams suggested that Dawkins "was misled by the fact that genes are always identified with DNA." For Williams, it was essential to be clear that the DNA molecule was the medium, not the message: the gene is "a package of information, not an object." Williams himself insisted that not all genes are evolutionary, if one defines an evolutionary gene as "any inherited information for which there is a favorable or unfavorable selection bias equal to several or many times its rate of endogenous change."[41]

So how does this work in practice? Perhaps the easiest way is to take a case study. Let's imagine a lion. The faster it can run, the more likely it is to survive – partly because it can outrun its prey, and hence ensure its food supply. Let's imagine that a genetic mutation takes place leading to a lion appearing with superior running skills. The local lion population now has two different kinds of lion: the ones with the new mutation, and the old ones without it. To begin with, they exist side by side. But the lions possessing this mutation have a greater capacity to survive, and hence pass their characteristics on to later generations through the gene – that is, whatever it is that caused this mutation in the first place.[42]

So how are these genetic mutations expressed in living organisms? At this point, we need to draw a distinction between the *gene* (or "genotype") as the "internally coded, inheritable information" carried by all living organisms, used as a "blueprint" or set of instructions for building and maintaining a living creature; and the *phenotype*, as the outward, physical manifestation of the organism – the visible characteristics or behavior which result from the interaction of an organism's genetic blueprint and the environment. Dawkins argues that the gene is the unit of selection, in that it exerts phenotypic effects on the organism – for example, the sharpness of its claws, the nature of its metabolism, or the strength of its leg muscles. Successful genes are those that cause phenotypic effects which promote their survival.

Dawkins took this a stage further through his ideas of an "extended phenotype."[43] He pointed out that the effects of the gene were not limited to physical characteristics of the individual organism, but extended to their environment. Bower birds construct grass structures within which to mate. Those species of bower birds with especially bright plumage tend to construct less elaborate bowers; those with less attractive plumage compensate for this by fabricating more intricate structures.[44]

This, then, is a brief sketch of Dawkins' approach, set against its historical background. There are problems with the approach, some arising from further advances in molecular biology – such as the publication of genome sequences – and others from questionable assumptions that appear to be embedded in his approach, and we may note one or two before proceeding further. We begin by considering some recent research that raises questions about the validity of the Darwinian "tree of life" model.

Dawkins' "tree of life" model, as presented in *The Blind Watchmaker*, sets out a simple Darwinian "descent with modification" formula using the idea of "perfect nesting."[45] Evolutionary descent demands a branching structure, similar to a genealogical tree. Yet recent work on genome sequencing of simple organisms, such as bacteria or archaea, seems to point to the repeated transfer of genes, or perhaps even clusters of genes, from organism to organism.[46] Most early studies assumed species evolved primarily by vertical inheritance from parent or parents. However, the comparison of microbial gene sequences suggests that horizontal inheritance may be relatively common. The growing evidence for extensive lateral gene transfer among organisms at the lower reaches of the tree of life[47] suggests that the image of a branching "tree of life" may need revision, to take account of this apparent intersection of rings close to its base.

It seems increasingly necessary to speak of a "Darwinian horizon" – a point way back in evolutionary time at which horizontal gene transfer was so common that the traditional Darwinian account becomes problematic. Darwinism, which posits vertical gene transfer as the dominant theme of evolution, can cope with lateral gene transfer as a subtext or sideshow; when it is the main story, however, things are rather more difficult. We shall have to wait and see how things develop here. I do not regard this as forcing a revision of Dawkins' overall approach; nevertheless, it alters the detail at some important points – not least by suggesting that the standard Darwinian account does not embrace the totality of evolutionary history.

Most criticism of Dawkins, however, has focused on the validity of the concept of "the selfish gene." Dawkins' phrase "the selfish gene" was criticized by philosopher Mary Midgley, partly because of what she regarded as definitional vagueness, but more fundamentally on account of philosophical laziness. "Genes cannot be selfish or unselfish, any more than atoms can be jealous, elephants abstract or biscuits teleological."[48] The basic concern expressed by Midgley was that the attribution of "selfishness" to genes represented a form of anthropomorphic thinking, by which genes were understood to possess human qualities and vices. Genes themselves cannot *be* selfish; the term can really only be applied meaningfully to an organism capable of behavior.[49] It was a reasonable point concerning the validity of metaphorical or analogical language. After all, can genes really be said to "behave" in any way, whether "selfish" or not? Genes replicate; they cannot be said to "behave" or "act," even in a pseudo-teleological way. This reasonable point was unfortunately lost in the noise of a scientifically confused piece of polemic which managed to misrepresent Dawkins' views on the gene.[50]

Yet Dawkins was no stranger to the use of analogies in the sciences. In his doctoral thesis he devoted several pages to exploring the proper use of models or "pictorial aids" in scientific explanation and description, especially in relation to issues of behavior.[51] Dawkins insisted that a clear distinction could be drawn between the subjective and behavioristic senses of the term, and that his definition was unequivocally behavioristic in nature. Genes behave *as if* they are selfish, whatever implications this may be understood to have. As he pointed out in *The Selfish Gene*, "we must not think of genes as conscious, purposeful agents. Blind natural selection, however, makes them behave rather as if they were purposeful, and it has been convenient, as a shorthand, to refer to genes in the language of purpose."[52] (Darwin himself, we may note, had earlier remarked that "natural selection" was "shorthand" for a much more complex and nuanced process.) Genes are not consciously selfish; yet their dynamics resemble those of consciously selfish agents.

Thus far, we have sketched the outlines of the Darwinian approach advocated by Dawkins. But what are its implications? What difference might it make to our broader view of reality, including that realm of human life and thought which is often, though somewhat misleadingly, called "religion"? In what follows, we shall explore some of the features of the Darwinian view of reality developed and so ably communicated by Dawkins.

## River out of Eden: Exploring a Darwinian world

For Dawkins, Darwin's theory of evolution – as developed in the light of Mendelian genetics and our understanding of the place of DNA in the transmission of inherited information – is more than a scientific theory. It is a worldview, a total account of reality. Darwinism is a "universal and timeless" principle, capable of being applied throughout the universe. In comparison, worldviews such as Marxism are "parochial and ephemeral."[53]

Where most evolutionary biologists would argue that Darwinism offers a *description* of reality, Dawkins insists that it offers more than this – it is an *explanation*.[54] Darwinism is a worldview, a *grand récit*, a metanarrative – a totalizing framework, by which the great questions of life are to be evaluated and answered. For this reason, Dawkins' account of things has provoked a response from postmodern writers, for whom any metanarrative – whether Marxist, Freudian, or Darwinian – is to be resisted as a matter of principle.[55]

So what is this worldview like? Let's note some of its leading features.

## A world without purpose

Jacques Monod's book *Chance and Necessity* (1972) caused something of a stir on its publication, chiefly on account of his total rejection of any purpose within the cosmos. All that Monod was doing was exploring the implications of a genetically driven account of reality, in which accidental changes were propagated by DNA, and subjected to the "teleonomic" filter of natural selection. Monod, then director of the Pasteur Institute in Paris, was particularly critical of the views of two fellow countrymen, Henri Bergson and Pierre Teilhard de Chardin, both of whom developed philosophies of life which were founded on acceptance of evolution, yet interpreted this as having some kind of purpose. A modern understanding of the molecular basis of evolution eliminated the notion of "purpose" altogether. Perhaps one could talk about the direction of the evolutionary process – but certainly not about its purpose. For Monod, *teleonomy* had displaced *teleology*. There was no point in asking why things had happened. They just had. While the mechanisms which governed evolution were of interest, they had no goal.

Dawkins echoes these ideas throughout his published works over the last twenty-five years. The natural sciences can clarify just about every aspect of the evolutionary mechanism; the pace of scientific progress is such that what is currently unexplained is unlikely to remain so for much longer. And when that mechanism is understood, the very notion of "purpose" had to be declared redundant. The world may appear to have been designed, or to have been created for some purpose. Yet this "strong illusion of purposeful design" can easily be explained on the basis of the outcome of chance mutations over huge periods of time. Dawkins is particularly critical of those who argue that, "since science is unable to answer 'Why' questions, there must be some other discipline that *is* qualified to answer them." No answer is possible, other than the Darwinian answer of natural selection.[56] We are here on account of no higher principle than natural selection, in that our distant forebears were able to increase the representation of their genes at the expense of others. There is no higher, no deeper, explanation of things than this.

To some, this seems a rather melancholy worldview. It might, of course, be reasonably pointed out that this is hardly an acceptable arbiter of whether something is right. I remember, during my days as an atheist, finding some solace in the fact that nobody could accuse me of being an atheist on account of the metaphysical comfort it brought. If it was right, it was an irrelevance whether it made its adherents gloomy or bright, nice or tedious. The issue was its relation to observed facts. For Dawkins, God has no "utility function" in explaining the way things are, and may safely be discarded as "very, very improbable indeed." (We'll come back to that later in the book, as the argument he offers here actually falls far short of that rather ambitious conclusion.)

Dawkins has a robustly positive take on Darwinism and the message that it brings to the world. In a short talk on BBC Radio in 2003, he set out his personal creed in the following terms.

[We should] rejoice in the amazing privilege we enjoy. We have been born, and we are going to die. But before we die we have time to understand why we were ever born in the first place. Time to understand the universe into which we have been born. And with that

44

understanding, we finally grow up and realize that there is no help for us outside our own efforts.[57]

Why were we ever born? The Darwinian answer is "natural selection." In fact, that's the Darwinian answer to just about everything.

But let's look at that answer to the question of why we – that is, human beings – are here. What are its implications?

## The place of humanity in a Darwinian universe

If there was one aspect of his own theory of evolution which left Charles Darwin feeling unsettled, it was its implications for the status and identity of the human race. In every edition of the *Origin of Species* Darwin consistently stated that his proposed mechanism of natural selection did not entail any fixed or universal law of progressive development. Furthermore, he explicitly rejected Lamarck's theory that evolution demonstrated an "innate and inevitable tendency towards perfection." The inevitable conclusion must therefore be that human beings (now understood to be participants within, rather than merely observers of, the evolutionary process) cannot in any sense be said to be either the "goal" or the "apex" of evolution. It was not an easy conclusion for Darwin, or for his age. The conclusion to the *Descent of Man* speaks of humanity in exalted terms, while insisting upon its "lowly" biological origins:

Man may be excused for feeling some pride at having risen, though not through his own exertions, to the very summit of the organic scale; and the fact of his having thus risen, instead of having been aboriginally placed there, may give him hope for a still higher destiny in the distant future. But we are not here concerned with hopes or fears, only with the truth as far as our reason permits us to discover it; and I have given the evidence to the best of my ability. We must, however, acknowledge, as it seems to me, that man with all his noble qualities . . . still bears in his bodily frame the indelible stamp of his lowly origin.[58]

Using his own version of the image of the "Great Chain of Being," Darwin occasionally seems to suggest that evolution implies progress towards superior creatures, projecting moral (and occasionally even ontological) qualities onto more neutral scientific description.[59]

Dawkins has no hesitations here. We must recognize that we are animals, part of the evolutionary process. He is strongly critical of the absolutist assumptions he discerns behind "speciesism" – a term invented by Richard Ryder, and given wider currency by Peter Singer, currently of Princeton University.[60]

Yet Dawkins draws an important – indeed, a remarkable – distinction between humanity and every other living product of genetic mutation and natural selection. *We alone are able to resist our genes.* While some writers – such as Julian Huxley – tried to develop an ethical system based on what they regarded as Darwinian evolution's more progressive aspects, Dawkins regards this as misguided.[61] Natural selection may be the dominant force in biological evolution; this does not for one moment mean that we need to endorse its apparent ethical implications.

It is an important point, as some have argued that Darwinian theory endorses a "survival of the fittest" ethic. A recently discovered letter of Darwin himself seems to lend credibility to this "social Darwinist" approach,[62] although Darwin is generally cautious about drawing any such conclusions. Dawkins is adamant: human beings are *not* the prisoner of their genes, but are capable of rebelling against such a genetic tyranny:

As an academic scientist I am a passionate Darwinian, believing that natural selection is, if not the only driving force in evolution, certainly the only known force capable of producing the illusion of purpose which so strikes all who contemplate nature. But at the same time as I support Darwinism as a scientist, I am a passionate anti-Darwinian when it comes to politics and how we should conduct our human affairs.[63]

This same theme emerges in *The Selfish Gene.* Dawkins concluded this work with a passionate defense of human dignity and freedom in the face of genetic determinism. We – that is, his (human) readers – can rebel:

We have the power to defy the selfish genes of our birth and, if necessary, the selfish memes of our indoctrination. We can even discuss ways of deliberately cultivating and nurturing pure, disinterested altruism – something that has no place in nature, something that has never existed before in the whole history of the world. We are built as gene machines and cultured as meme machines, but we have the power to turn against our creators. We, alone on earth, can rebel against the tyranny of the selfish replicators.[64]

(Note that Dawkins introduces the term "meme" here, as a "cultural replicator" analogous to the gene, as a genetic replicator. We shall have more to say about this new type of replicator later.) Dawkins suggests that the situation can be compared to an oncologist, whose professional specialty is *studying* cancer, and whose professional vocation is *fighting* it.

So there *is* something different about humanity, after all. We alone appear to have evolved to the point at which we are able to rebel against precisely the process that brought us here in the first place. Only we have evolved brains which are capable of, in the first place, understanding how we came to be here, and in the second, subverting the process that may at some very distant point lead to our being displaced, perhaps by some superior primate.

The evolution of the human brain is, as Dawkins points out, as remarkable as it is controversial. What pressures led to the enlargement of the human brain?[65] And why should this process yield any significant evolutionary advantage? This new development requires that roughly one quarter of human metabolism is devoted to ensuring brain function. This represents a substantial investment of energy, and a correspondingly high risk for the survival of the species. Nevertheless, whatever its explanation, it happened.[66]

By wise use of this additional resource, humans alone can subvert their "selfish genes" – for example, through using artificial contraception.[67] It's a moot point whether this example can be regarded as a brave act of rebellion by enlightened humans against their genes. It could equally be argued to be an act of collusion. One of the driving arguments for artificial contraception is that it limits the disastrous consequences of population explosion, which would pose a challenge to the continued existence of the human species – and hence the transmission of the human gene.

In this chapter, I have introduced Dawkins' characteristic notion of the "selfish gene," setting it within the context of the development of evolutionary biology since Darwin. This allows us to move on to the real agenda of this book: to offer a critical examination of Dawkins' assessment of its religious implications. To explore this important question, we may turn immediately to consider one of Dawkins' most important works: *The Blind Watchmaker.*

# The Blind Watchmaker: Evolution and the Elimination of God?

Darwin marks the parting of the ways. He is the colossus who separates two radically different ways of thinking. Robert Green Ingersoll (1833–99), the railroad lawyer who became one of America's most prominent nineteenth-century atheist writers, had no hesitation in foretelling the triumph of Darwin over all forms of religious faith. Writing in 1884, Ingersoll declared:

This century will be called Darwin's century . . . His doctrine of evolution, his doctrine of the survival of the fittest, his doctrine of the origin of species, has removed in every thinking mind the last vestige of orthodox Christianity.

As things turned out, Christianity managed to survive Ingersoll's prophecies of doom. Yet the issue remains: is Darwinism, as both Ingersoll and Dawkins insist, *necessarily* atheistic?

Before Darwin, Dawkins argues, it was possible to see the world as something designed by God; after Darwin, we can speak only of the "illusion of design." A Darwinian world has no purpose, and we delude ourselves if we think otherwise. If the universe cannot be described as "good," at least it cannot be described as "evil" either.

In a universe of blind physical forces and genetic replication, some people are going to get hurt, other people are going to get lucky, and you won't find any rhyme or reason in it, nor any justice. The universe we observe had precisely the properties we should expect if there is, at bottom, no design, no purpose, no evil and no good, nothing but blind pitiless indifference.[1]

But some insist that there does indeed seem to be a "purpose" to things, and cite the apparent design of things in support. Surely, such critics argue, the intricate structure of the human eye points to something that cannot be explained by natural forces, and which obliges us to invoke a divine creator by way of explanation? How otherwise may we explain the vast and complex structures that we observe in nature?[2]

Dawkins' answer is set out primarily in two works: *The Blind Watchmaker* and *Climbing Mount Improbable*. The fundamental argument common to both is that complex things evolve from simple beginnings, over long periods of time.

Living things are too improbable and too beautifully "designed" to have come into existence by chance. How, then, did they come into existence? The answer, Darwin's answer, is by gradual, step-by-step transformations from simple beginnings, from primordial entities sufficiently simple to have come into existence by chance. Each successful change in the gradual evolutionary process was simple enough, *relative to its predecessor*, to have arisen by chance. But the whole sequence of cumulative steps constitutes anything but a chance process.[3]

What might seem to be a highly improbable development needs to be set against the backdrop of the huge periods of time envisaged by the evolutionary process. Dawkins explores this point using the image of a metaphorical "Mount Improbable." Seen from one angle, its "towering, vertical cliffs" seem impossible to climb. Yet, seen from another angle, the mountain turns out to have "gently inclined grassy meadows, graded steadily and easily towards the distant uplands."[4]

The "illusion of design," Dawkins argues, arises because we intuitively regard structures as being too complex to have arisen by chance. An excellent example is provided by the human eye, cited by some advocates of the divine design and direct special creation of the world as a surefire proof of God's existence. In one of the most detailed and argumentative chapters of *Climbing Mount Improbable*, Dawkins shows how, given enough time, even such a complex organ could have evolved from something much simpler.[5]

It's all standard Darwinism. What's new is the lucidity of the presentation, and the detailed illustration and defense of these ideas through judiciously selected case studies and carefully crafted analogies. In that Dawkins sees Darwinism as a worldview, rather than a biological theory, he has no hesitation in taking his arguments far beyond the bounds of the purely biological. The word "God" is absent from the index of *The Blind Watchmaker* precisely because he is absent from the Darwinian world that Dawkins inhabits and commends.[6] The evolutionary process leaves no conceptual space for God. What an earlier generation explained by an appeal to a divine creator can be accommodated within a Darwinian framework. There is no need to believe in God after Darwin.

But Dawkins is not going to leave things there. Some might draw the conclusion that Darwinism encourages agnosticism. Far from it: for Dawkins, Darwin impels us to atheism. It is not merely that evolution erodes the explanatory potency of God; it eliminates God altogether. In an important essay of 1996, Dawkins argues that there are at present only three possible ways of seeing the world: Darwinism, Lamarckism, or God.[7] The last two fail to explain the world; the only option is therefore Darwinism.

I'm a Darwinist because I believe the only alternatives are Lamarckism or God, neither of which does the job as an explanatory principle. Life in the universe is either Darwinian or something else not yet thought of.

Now the rhetoric of his argument demands that Darwinism, Lamarckism, and belief in God are three mutually exclusive views, so that commitment to one necessarily entails rejection of the others. Yet it is well known that many Darwinians believe that there is a convergence between Darwinism and theism. The extent of that overlap is most certainly open to discussion, and it is far from being a settled issue. Yet Dawkins' conclusion depends upon proposing an absolute dichotomy – *either* Darwinism *or* God – when the theories themselves do not require such absolutist ways of thinking (though they certainly permit it).

Dawkins has certainly demonstrated that a purely natural *description* may be offered of what is currently known of the history and present state of living organisms. But *why* does this lead to the conclusion that there is no God? A host of unstated and unchallenged assumptions underlie his argument. In this chapter, we shall explore a series of objections which might be brought against Dawkins' conclusion. To summarize them briefly:

1 At the most general level, the scientific method is incapable of adjudicating the God hypothesis, either positively or negatively.

2 Dawkins' arguments lead to the conclusion that God need not be invoked as an explanatory agent within the evolutionary process. This is consistent with various atheist, agnostic, and Christian understandings of the world, but necessitates none of them.

3 The concept of God as "watchmaker," which Dawkins spends so much time demolishing, emerged as significant in the eighteenth century, and is not typical of the Christian tradition. It was developed by Robert Boyle (1627–91), who compared the universe to the Great Clock of Strasbourg. Initially applied to the physical aspects of the world, the analogy was transferred to the biological sphere in the late eighteenth century. What Dawkins demonstrates is the vulnerability of a historically contingent approach to the doctrine of creation, linked with the specific historical circumstances of eighteenth-century England, which had already been rejected as inadequate, possibly even unorthodox, by many leading English theologians of the time.

If these considerations have any cumulative force, they lead to an important conclusion: Dawkins' atheism is inadequately grounded in the biological evidence. Therefore we must seek its ultimate grounds elsewhere. In what follows, we shall consider each of these points individually.

## Natural Science Leads Neither to Atheism Nor Christianity

The scientific method is incapable of delivering a decisive adjudication of the God question. Those who believe that it proves or disproves the existence of God press that method beyond its legitimate limits, and run the risk of abusing or discrediting it. Some distinguished biologists (such as Francis S. Collins, director of the Human Genome Project) argue that the natural sciences create a positive presumption of faith;[8] others (such as the evolutionary biologist Stephen Jay Gould) that they have negative implications for theistic belief. But they *prove* nothing, either way. If the God question is to be settled, it must be settled on other grounds.

This is not a new idea. Indeed, the recognition of the religious limits of the scientific method was well understood around the time of Darwin himself. As none other than "Darwin's Bulldog," T. H. Huxley, wrote in 1880:[9]

Some twenty years ago, or thereabouts, I invented the word "Agnostic" to denote people who, like myself, confess themselves to be hopelessly ignorant concerning a variety of matters, about which metaphysicians and theologians, both orthodox and heterodox, dogmatize with utmost confidence.

Fed up with both theists and atheists making hopelessly dogmatic statements on the basis of inadequate empirical evidence, Huxley declared that the God question could not be settled on the basis of the scientific method.

Agnosticism is of the essence of science, whether ancient or modern. It simply means that a man shall not say he knows or believes that which he has no scientific grounds for professing to know or

Plate 6    Thomas Henry Huxley (1825–95). Photo AKG-Images

believe . . . Consequently Agnosticism puts aside not only the greater part of popular theology, but also the greater part of anti-theology.

Huxley's arguments are as valid today as they were in the late nineteenth century, despite the protestations of those on both sides of the great debate about God.

In a 1992 critique of an anti-evolutionary work which posited that Darwinism was *necessarily* atheistic,[10] Stephen Jay Gould invoked the memory of Mrs. McInerney, his third grade teacher, who was in the habit of rapping young knuckles when their owners said or did particularly stupid things:

To say it for all my colleagues and for the umpteenth millionth time (from college bull sessions to learned treatises): science simply cannot (by its legitimate methods) adjudicate the issue of God's possible superintendence of nature. We neither affirm nor deny it; we simply can't comment on it as scientists. If some of our crowd have made untoward statements claiming that Darwinism disproves God, then I will find Mrs. McInerney and have their knuckles rapped for it (as long as she can equally treat those members of our crowd who have argued that Darwinism must be God's method of action).

Gould rightly insists that science can work only with naturalistic explanations; it can neither affirm nor deny the existence of God. The bottom line for Gould is that Darwinism actually has no bearing on the existence or nature of God. If Darwinians choose to dogmatize on matters of religion, they stray beyond the straight and narrow way of the scientific method, and end up in the philosophical badlands. Either a conclusion cannot be reached at all on such matters, or it is to be reached on other grounds.

Now Dawkins knows perfectly well that "science has no way to disprove the existence of a supreme being."[11] This, he argues, cannot be allowed to lead to the conclusion that "belief (or disbelief) in a supreme being is a matter of pure individual inclination." But who said anything about "pure individual inclination"? Where does this idea come from? Dawkins seems to imply that, where the scientific method cannot be properly applied, there is only epistemological anarchy. Without the scientific method, we are reduced to the pure subjectivity of individual opinion.

This misleading gloss on a perfectly serious and legitimate debate about the limits of the scientific method allows Dawkins to evade the point at issue. If the scientific method can neither prove nor disprove the existence or nature of God, then either we abandon the question as unanswerable (something Dawkins certainly does not choose to do) or we answer it on other grounds.

But the point at issue cannot be sidestepped in this way. If an answer is to be given, it is not a matter of "pure individual inclination," but of reasoned and principled argument on the basis of whatever criteria of judgment apply to this debate. This is not an arbitrary or whimsical matter, but a matter of intellectual integrity, in which all sides to the debate – whether atheist, theist, or Christian – seek to offer the "best explanation" of the available evidence.[12] This is basic philosophy of science, and it is not going to go away because Dawkins ignores it.

The issue emerges as important on account of the problem of "underdetermination of theory by evidence." At times, it is impossible to adjudicate between rival theories precisely because they seem to offer equally good accounts of observation. Two quite different theories may turn out to be "empirically equivalent," forcing the scientific community to suspend judgment until the issue is resolved by evidence, or reaching a decision on other grounds. An excellent example is provided by two rival schools of quantum mechanics: the "Copenhagen school," based on the approach of Niels Bohr and Werner Heisenberg, and that of David Bohm.[13] The two are empirically equivalent, and arguably equally elegant and simple.

In practice, the Copenhagen approach has achieved dominance – but largely on account of issues of historical contingency, not theoretical superiority. The two theories are associated with quite different worldviews, with the Copenhagen approach favoring an essentially indeterminist universe, and the Bohmian approach a more determinist model. Much depends on the theory choice made; yet the choice cannot be made with conviction. As James Cushing points out, this hasn't stopped people from making choices. Yet the scientific legitimacy of such decisions is open to question. Either we cannot reach a decision, or we must reach that decision on other grounds.

Yet if the scientific method cannot settle an issue, it does not mean that all answers have to be regarded as equally valid, or that we abandon rationality in order to deal with them. It simply means that the discussion shifts to another level, using different criteria of evidence and argumentation. As it happens, that is precisely what Dawkins does himself – develop arguments for atheism which are ultimately non-scientific in character. We shall return to consider how successful these are in due course. But the key point for the moment is simply this: the scientific method *alone* cannot ultimately determine the

God question, even though it has some important contributions to make to the debate.

Let's move on, and look at another aspect of the debate over the theological implications of Darwinism.

## God as an Explanatory Hypothesis

Dawkins argues that God is redundant as an explanatory hypothesis. God has no discernible "utility function" in scientific explanation. In support of this idea, he offers a number of arguments, of which the most interesting is his "biomorph programme."[14] This analogy is intended to help us appreciate that the *appearance* of design can arise from random developments. Imagine, he suggests, a monkey (or equivalent) with a typewriter equipped with twenty-six capital letters and a space bar. Dawkins selects a twenty-eight character phrase from Shakespeare's *Hamlet*, as follows:

METHINKS IT IS LIKE A WEASEL

This is the "target phrase." Now, a computer generates, at random, a phrase of twenty-eight characters – the equivalent of the proverbial monkey trying to type out the works of Shakespeare. Needless to say, it bears no relation to the target phrase.

But now something happens. The computer has been instructed to examine the phrase, and select the one "which, *however slightly*, most resembles the target phrase."[15] The process now continues. After a mere thirty iterations, something recognizably like the target phrase has developed:

METHINGS IT IS LIKE I WEASEL

Just a dozen or so iterations later, and the target phrase has been reached. Dawkins concludes that the process of evolution is capable of bringing about the appearance of order rather more quickly and effectively than might be expected.

The analogy, however, is flawed. Indeed, it is an excellent example of what Friedrich Waismann termed the "conjuring away of philosophical problems" through carefully controlled and selected analogies.[16] The most obvious problem is that the analogy presupposes a teleology which Dawkins believes to be absent in nature. There is no "target phrase" towards which evolution may proceed. Dawkins concedes this point in the same work, but does not regard it as being critical to his analogy.[17]

Yet there is another problem, which Dawkins does not properly address. The idea of design or purposeful selection has been eliminated only at the *verbal* level. While the analogy allows us to avoid the vocabulary of "design," the notion of design is implicit in the computer program, which was constructed to control the development in a certain specific way. An unacknowledged anthropomorphism underlies the analogy, and lends it plausibility for the intended readership. Remove the (designed) computer program and the analogy loses much of its plausibility. It is best seen simply and solely as an indication of how small random mutations can accumulate to yield substantial changes *provided that they are selected non-randomly.*[18]

Setting to one side the plausibility of the analogy, let us focus on the point that Dawkins wants to make. A "theory of random mutation plus non-random cumulative selection" can explain the appearance of design in the world. There is no need to posit a God as an explanatory mechanism. Suppose we concede this point; what are its implications? Dawkins infers that, since God may be ignored as an improbable irrelevance, the only meaningful position is atheism. Yet he does not actually make the logical moves required to reach such a conclusion, apparently assuming that they are so self-evident that they do not require demonstration. But it is not so. To illustrate this point, we may explore the view of the world set out by the leading Christian theologian Thomas Aquinas in the thirteenth century.

Aquinas constructed a framework for understanding God's relation to the world which weaves together the fundamental themes of the Christian creeds.[19] The basic ideas that Aquinas developed can be set out very simply, as follows. God is the cause of all things. Yet God's causality operates in a number of ways. While God must be considered capable of doing certain things directly, God delegates causal efficacy to the created order. For Aquinas, this notion of secondary causality must be considered as an extension of, not an alternative to, the primary causality of God himself. Events within the created order can exist in complex causal relationships, without in any way denying their ultimate dependency upon God as final cause.

The critical point to appreciate is that the created order thus demonstrates causal relationships which can be investigated by the natural sciences. Those causal relationships can be investigated and correlated – for example, in the form of the "laws of nature" – without in any way implying, still less necessitating, an atheist worldview. To put this as simply as possible: God creates a world with its own ordering and processes.

This classic approach had its strengths and weaknesses. The most obvious of its strengths is that it laid the conceptual foundations for the development of the natural sciences in the later Middle Ages, by encouraging the investigation of natural processes and events. It is, by the way, important to note that this Christian view of the world was set out long before Darwin. As a result, there is no way that Aquinas' approach can be described as a *post hoc* attempt to defend Christianity in response to a perceived threat from the new science of evolutionary biology.

A potential weakness of this approach was that the self-regulation of the natural order could lead to God being conceptually marginalized in any account of the world. An explanation of the orbits of the planets could be offered, for example, which made no reference to God. As Pierre-Simon Laplace (1749–1827) pointed out in his massive *Treatise of Celestial Mechanics*, a self-sustaining mechanism effectively eliminated the need for God either as explanatory hypothesis or as active sustainer in cosmology. Yet for many, this was an acceptable risk.

Precisely this conceptual marginalization of the divine can be seen in Darwin's account of natural selection. What Darwin offered the readers of his *Origin of Species* was an explanation of the origins and present geographical distribution of biological species which operated entirely in terms of secondary causality. Dawkins interprets this as at least eliminating, and more probably discrediting, the existence of God. In his own writings, he offers a more advanced Darwinian explanation of biological diversity, with particular emphasis being placed on the molecular basis of the evolutionary process. Once more, the conclusion is that God is superfluous; the observational data may be explained without needing to invoke divine agency.

Christian natural scientists regard the God hypothesis as giving new insights and added depth to their engagement with, and appreciation of, nature. Others prefer to explain the world *etsi Deus non daretur* ("as if God were not given"), to use a phrase popularized by the Dutch jurist Hugo Grotius (1583–1645). Yet the alleged explanatory superfluity of God clearly has no bearing on the question of his existence. It is consistent with Christian, agnostic, and atheist accounts of the world. If there is an argument to be made against God, that must have its origins elsewhere.

## The Case of William Paley

*The Blind Watchmaker* represents a significant and highly successful attack on the eighteenth-century concept of God as a "watchmaker." But what are the implications of this? The view that Dawkins demolishes became significant only in the eighteenth century, and is not typical of the Christian tradition as a whole. It was a hasty response to the intellectual challenge of what is usually known as "the mechanical philosophy."[20] Initially applied to the physical world, the "watchmaker" analogy was transposed to the biological sphere in the late eighteenth century, with results that some found reassuring, and others deeply unsatisfying.

What Dawkins actually demonstrates is that a very specific understanding of the doctrine of creation, which came into being in response to the historical circumstances of eighteenth-century England, is completely undermined by a Darwinian account of evolution. This theory, associated with William Paley (1743–1805), archdeacon of Carlisle, had already been rejected as inadequate by many leading theologians of the day – such as John Henry Newman (1801–90) – before Darwin undermined it still further. In view of the importance of this point, we shall examine Paley's theory in some detail.

The background to William Paley's emphasis on the apparent "contrivance" of the biological world is a peculiarly English affair, arising through the complex interaction of politics and religion in England in the early eighteenth century. This development is fascinating historically, as well as being of no small importance to Dawkins' thesis of the "blind watchmaker."[21]

In the late seventeenth century, a series of events within both the British state and society at large forced the Church of England onto the defensive. One of these is of particular relevance for our purposes: the emergence of "Deism," a view of God which recognizes the divine creatorship, yet which rejects any continuing divine involvement with the world. The rise of Deism caused some problems for the established church, especially in relation to how the Bible and doctrinal tradition of the church were to be interpreted. Impressed by Isaac Newton's demonstration of the mechanical regularity of the world, many within the church began to explore the idea that an appeal to the natural world might be the basis for a new defense of Christian ideas.[22]

Now an interest in the natural world has always been part of the Christian intellectual tradition. However, in the past, this generally took the form of interpreting the world from a Christian perspective, appealing to the wonder and beauty of the natural world as a way of appreciating the beauty of God.[23] It is well known that one of the most fundamental impulses leading to the development of the natural sciences in the sixteenth and seventeenth centuries was the belief that to study nature at close quarters was to gain a deeper appreciation of the wisdom of God.[24] As the great naturalist John Ray (1628–1705) – author of the celebrated work *The Wisdom of God Manifested in the Works of Creation* (1691) – put it in 1660:

There is for a free man no occupation more worthy and delightful than to contemplate the beauteous works of nature and honour the infinite wisdom and goodness of God.

61

Yet all this changed in the early eighteenth century. A new approach to doing theology developed, which would be variously known as "natural theology" or "physical theology" (from the Greek word *physis*, "nature"). The existence and attributes of God, it was argued, could be inferred from nature itself. As rationalism gained a growing hold on English intellectual life, the established church responded by shifting emphasis from traditional sources of authority (such as the Bible) to the natural world. The existence and wisdom of God could be proved to an increasingly skeptical world by an appeal to the ordering of nature.

Initially, this "natural theology" made its appeal to the ordering of the physical world – and above all, to the regularity of the "celestial mechanics" demonstrated by Isaac Newton. Suddenly, Newton was seen as having mapped out a new approach to defending Christianity and doing theology. "Physical theology" became all the rage in the early 1700s. Yet it was not long before what had seemed to be a promising alliance between science and religion led to a growing and potentially irreversible estrangement.[25] An approach once advocated by the leading scientists of the day passed into the decidedly less competent hands of bishops and archdeacons, who often repeated at second hand ideas they had not properly understood, and whose implications they were prone to exaggerate. The Newtonian system seemed to many to suggest that the world was a self-sustaining mechanism which had no need for divine governance or sustenance for its day-to-day operation.[26] Far from encouraging belief in God, it declared this to be quite unnecessary.

By the end of the eighteenth century, it seemed to many that Newton's system probably led to atheism or agnosticism, rather than to faith. By 1750 it was becoming obvious that Newton's synthesis of the physical sciences and religion had failed. Its death blow came when Percy Bysshe Shelley famously remarked "the consistent Newtonian is necessarily an atheist."[27]

But long before then, others had turned to the world of biology. If physics was a dead end, might it be possible to construct arguments for God's existence based on an appeal to the living world of nature, rather than the regular orbits of the planets? It would prove to be the last stand of an intellectual movement that was in terminal decline. It was an experiment in Christian apologetics – the discipline that concerns itself with responding to objections that may be raised to Christian faith – that had gone wrong, and should have been abandoned. But Paley could see a way of injecting new life into the approach. It would live to fight another day. As it happened, Paley's approach achieved a popular success beyond anything he could have imagined. Yet it created the utterly false impression that the intellectual credibility of Christianity somehow depended upon the approach he adopted. The approach? God as the watchmaker.

Paley's *Natural Theology; or Evidences of the Existence and Attributes of the Deity, Collected from the Appearances of Nature* (1802) had a profound influence on popular English religious thought in the first half of the nineteenth century, and is known to have been read by Charles Darwin. Paley was deeply impressed by Newton's discovery of the regularity of nature, especially in relation to the area usually known as "celestial mechanics." It was clear that the entire universe could be thought of as a complex mechanism, operating according to regular and understandable principles.

For Paley, the analogy of God as a watchmaker needed to be transferred from the physical to the biological domain. Nature was to be seen as a "contrivance." This important word implies the ideas of *design* and *construction* – both of which Paley held to be evident in the biological world. Paley argues that only someone who is mad would suggest that complex mechanical technology came into being by purposeless chance. Mechanism presupposes contrivance – that is to say, both a sense of purpose and an ability to design and fabricate. Both the human body in particular, and the world in general, could be seen as mechanisms which had been designed and constructed, perfectly adapted to their needs and specific situations.

The opening paragraphs of Paley's *Natural Theology* set out the analogy for which Paley became famous, and which is the subject of many gracious, yet ultimately critical, references within Dawkins' *Blind Watchmaker*:

Plate 7    William Paley (1743–1805) © CORBIS

In crossing a heath, suppose I pitched my foot against a *stone*, and were asked how the stone came to be there. I might possibly answer, that for any thing I knew to the contrary it had lain there for ever; nor would it, perhaps, be very easy to show the absurdity of this answer. But suppose I had found a *watch* upon the ground, and it should be inquired how the watch happened to be in that place. I should hardly think of the answer which I had before given, that for any thing I knew the watch might have always been there. Yet why should this answer not serve for the watch as well as for the stone; why is it not admissible in the second case as in the first?[28]

Paley then offers a detailed description of the watch, noting in particular its container, coiled cylindrical spring, many interlocking wheels, and glass face. Having carried his readers along with this careful analysis, Paley turns to draw his critically important conclusion:

This mechanism being observed – it requires indeed an examination of the instrument, and perhaps some previous knowledge of the subject, to perceive and understand it; but being once, as we have said, observed and understood, the inference we think is inevitable, that the watch must have had a maker – that there must have existed, at some time and at some place or other, an artificer or artificers who formed it for the purpose which we find it actually to answer, who comprehended its construction and designed its use.

The analogy, like most of Paley's work, was borrowed, and the scholarship decidedly second rate. Paley had ruthlessly plagiarized John Ray's writings in his quest for a new natural theology. Though a derivative and old-fashioned thinker, Paley was still an excellent communicator. What he communicated so effectively was nevertheless an outmoded way of thinking. Nature, Paley argued, shows signs of "contrivance" – that is, purposeful design and fabrication. Nature bears witness to a series of biological structures which are "contrived" – that is, constructed with a clear purpose in mind. "Every indication of contrivance, every manifestation of design, which existed in the watch, exists in the works of nature." Indeed, Paley argues, nature shows an even greater degree of contrivance than the watch. He is at his best when dealing with the immensely complex structures of the human eye and heart, each of which can be described in mechanical terms. Anyone using a telescope, he points out, knows that the instrument was designed and manufactured. Who, he wonders, can look at the human eye, and fail to see that it also has a designer?

Dawkins himself is eloquent and generous in his account of Paley's achievement, noting with appreciation his "beautiful and reverent descriptions of the dissected machinery of life."[29] Without in any way belittling the wonder of the mechanical "watches" that so fascinated and impressed Paley, Dawkins

argued that his case for God – though made with "passionate
sincerity" and "informed by the best biological scholarship of
his day" – is "gloriously and utterly wrong." The "only watchmaker in nature is the blind forces of physics."

Thus Dawkins; but what about Darwin? Although scholarly
investigation of the evolution of Darwin's ideas has uncovered
new and potentially significant connections with alternative
approaches to natural theology in the 1830s and 1840s,[30] there
is no doubt of the lingering influence of Paley on Darwin. As
an undergraduate at Cambridge University, Charles Darwin
read Paley, and was impressed by his arguments. At that time,
Paley was widely read at Cambridge.[31]

[Paley's] *Natural Theology* gave me as much delight as did Euclid.
The careful study of these works, without attempting to learn any
part by rote, was the only part of the Academical Course which, as
I then felt and as I still believe, was of the least use to me in the
education of my mind. I did not at that time trouble myself about
Paley's premises; and taking these on trust I was charmed and convinced of the long line of argumentation.

Yet he was aware of some problems within Paley's scheme,
even without recourse to evolutionary theory.

Paley's argument emphasized the wisdom of God in creation.
But what, Darwin wondered, of God's goodness? How could
the brutality, pain, and sheer waste of nature be reconciled
with the idea of a benevolent God? In his "Sketch of 1842"
Darwin found himself pondering how such things as "creeping
parasites" and other creatures that lay their eggs in the bowels
or flesh of other animals can be justified within Paley's scheme.
How could God's goodness be reconciled with such less pleas-
ant aspects of the created order?

There can be no doubt of the influence of Paley on Darwin.
Even in his later writings, Darwin tended to use "the patterns
of speech, the argumentative structures, and the basic concepts
of Paley as if they were his own."[32] Yet Darwin had no doubt
that his theory of natural selection disposed of Paley's theory
of "physical theology" or "physico-theology." Deliberately
mimicking Paley's vocabulary, Darwin insisted that what an

earlier generation of naturalists might reasonably have regarded as "contrivances" – that is, deliberately designed features – could now be seen as having evolved *naturally*. Darwin developed this point most fully in a work published in 1862, entitled *On the various contrivances by which British and foreign orchids are fertilised by insects*. The deliberate use of the word "contrivance" here must be seen as a direct, explicit criticism of Paley. The orchids, Darwin explains, possess many "beautiful contrivances," which some interpret "as the result of the direct interposition of the Creator." Others, he suggests, might now wish to see these same contrivances as "due to secondary laws." In many ways, Dawkins' *Blind Watchmaker* can be seen as an expansion of the argument of this 1862 writing of Darwin, set within a neo-Darwinian framework. The science may have moved on, but the religious conclusions are the same: natural processes and laws explain apparent design.

Yet others had their misgivings about Paley on theological grounds, and were not slow to express them. Before Darwin's new theory made its appearance, a growing body of informed theological opinion was urging the abandoning of Paley's ideas, or their significant modification. In 1852 John Henry Newman was invited to give a series of lectures in Dublin on "the idea of a university." This allowed him to explore the relation between Christianity and the sciences, and especially the "physical theology" of William Paley. Newman was scathing about Paley's approach, lambasting it as "a false gospel." Far from being an advance on the more modest approaches adopted by the early church, it represented a degradation of those ideas.

The nub of Newman's criticism can be summarized in a sentence: "It has been taken out of its place, has been put too prominently forward, and thereby has almost been used as an instrument against Christianity."[33] Paley's "physical theology" was a liability, and ought to be abandoned before it discredited Christianity.

Physical Theology cannot, from the nature of the case, tell us one word about Christianity proper; it cannot be Christian, in any true

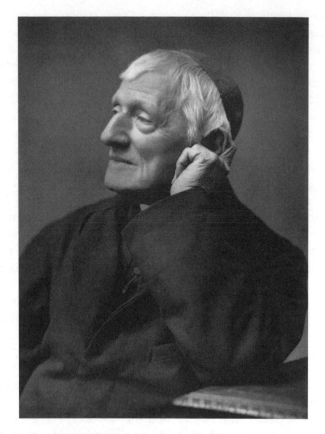

Plate 8    John Henry Newman (1801–90) © Hulton-Deutsch Collection/CORBIS

sense, at all . . . Nay, more than this; I do not hesitate to say that, taking men as they are, this so-called science tends, if it occupies the mind, to dispose it against Christianity.[34]

Seven years before Darwin subverted Paley's approach on scientific grounds, Newman – widely regarded as the most important English theologian of the nineteenth century – had repudiated Paley as an outdated theological liability.

What is interesting is that there is no awareness on Newman's part of a new crisis of faith about to be precipitated by Darwin's work. His argument, which predates Darwin's *Origin of Species*, rests solely on his belief that Paley's approach fails in what it sought to deliver, and traps Christian theology in an apologetic which can only go disastrously wrong. It was not the first time Christian apologetics had taken a disastrous wrong turn; an immediate correction was, in Newman's view, long overdue.

Others, however, took the view that Darwin's theory of evolution allowed Paley to be developed in more helpful directions. As James Moore has shown in his massive and definitive account of Christian responses to Darwin, there were many who believed that the obvious deficiencies in Paley's account of biological life – most notably, the notion of "perfect adaptation" – were corrected by Darwin's notion of natural selection.[35] More importantly, a series of writers discarded Paley's interest in specific adaptations (to use a Darwinian term unknown to him), and preferred to focus on the fact that evolution appeared to be governed by certain quite definite laws – a clear application to biology of the general approach developed in the Middle Ages by Aquinas. An excellent example of this is R. S. S. Baden-Powell's *Essays on the Spirit of the Inductive Philosophy* (1855), written before Darwin's theory forced reconsideration of the issue through its new approach to the natural world.[36]

Paley must be seen in his historical context. He represents the late and final flowering of a movement that came into being in the aftermath of the great Newtonian revolution of the late seventeenth century, and which had completely lost its way by the middle of the eighteenth century. Paley simply reworked older ideas, unaware that their already tenuous credibility was about to expire. Darwin's *Origin of Species* and later writings must be seen as a nineteenth-century refutation of an eighteenth-century idea – an idea already rejected by leading Christian writers of the age. But it cannot be regarded as a refutation of Christianity itself – merely of a wrong turn that the English national church took.

Christianity is not a static entity; rather, it is like a growing plant.[37] Although grounded in the Bible, the Christian theological tradition has always been mindful of the need to interpret its foundational text in the most authentic way possible. This has led to debates within the church over how best to interpret certain passages. In the first 500 years of Christianity, a number of basic principles emerged. One of these was to interpret the Bible in such a way that allowed a creative interaction with the best natural science of the day.

The most influential theologian of this era was Augustine of Hippo (354–430), who is of especial importance in relation to the exploration of the relationship between biblical interpretation and the sciences. Augustine stressed the importance of respecting the conclusions of the sciences in relation to biblical exegesis. As Augustine observed in his commentary on Genesis, certain of its passages were genuinely open to diverse interpretations. It was therefore important to allow further scientific research to assist in the determination of which was the most appropriate mode of interpretation for a given passage:[38]

In matters that are so obscure and far beyond our vision, we find in Holy Scripture passages which can be interpreted in very different ways without prejudice to the faith we have received. In such cases, we should not rush in headlong and so firmly take our stand on one side that, if further progress in the search for truth justly undermines our position, we too fall with it. We should not battle for our own interpretation but for the teaching of the Holy Scripture. We should not wish to conform the meaning of Holy Scripture to our interpretation, but our interpretation to the meaning of Holy Scripture.

Augustine therefore urged that biblical interpretation should take due account of what could reasonably be regarded as established facts. This approach to biblical interpretation aimed to ensure that Christian theology never became trapped in a pre-scientific worldview. This has always been the dominant theme in Western biblical interpretation. Yet it does not preclude debates over what is the best approach. And these debates often involved trial and error, determining the best way of interpreting a biblical passage by an extended period of discussion and exploration.

And one of those explorations was due to William Paley. It does not matter that history regards it as one of the less successful pieces of theological adventurism. We cannot adopt a "Whig view of history," which lauds those explorations which succeeded, and excoriates those which failed. To use Arnold Toynbee's famous phrase, the whole enterprise of Christian theology, like human civilization itself, is "a movement and not a condition, a voyage and not a harbor." Precisely the same is true of the scientific method. Exploration is essential. Evaluation of Paley's approach to Christian apologetics was under way from 1800, and was essentially complete by 1850, before the publication of Darwin's theory. The verdict? It was an experiment that had failed. It was time to rediscover older approaches to apologetics, and develop new ones, untainted by the failures of Paley. Yet such was Paley's impact that his ideas lingered within Victorian culture – and with them, an essentially static understanding of the biological world, which was improperly assumed to be *the* Christian view of things. No wonder that so many theologians wanted to get back to an earlier, more authentic way of doing theology, and set Paley's adventurism to one side.

Dawkins' assessment of the theological implications of Darwinism is excessively dependent on the assumption that Paley (or Paleyesque) approaches to the biosphere are typical or normative for Christianity. He also seems to assume that the intellectual case for Christianity rests largely, if not totally, upon an "argument for design," such as that proposed by Paley. Yet Christian theology does not hold that Christian belief is irrational or lacking positive epistemic status without the kind of arguments that Paley develops. Dawkins makes a superb case for abandoning Paley. Sadly, he seems to think this also entails abandoning God.

So what if we were to forget about Paley, and return to the biblical interpretation and theological methods of the early church? Sadly, this is a historical experiment which simply cannot be undertaken. History, like the evolutionary process described by Darwin and Dawkins, is irreversible, and prone to contingencies which lie beyond experimental control. Happenstance is as important in cultural as it is in biological evolution. But what can be said, and needs to be said, is this: if the Darwinian debate had taken place in the Greek-speaking church of the fourth century, things would have worked out very differently.[39] The criticism I therefore wish to make is this: Dawkins' strongly negative assessment of the religious implications of Darwinism depends on depicting a local historical

71

contingency as a universal theological necessity. Even allowing for the cultural importance of Britain in the nineteenth century, you cannot present the local conditions of Victorian England as if they were determinant of the Christian faith down the ages.

Thus far, I have raised three objections to Dawkins' analysis of the implications of Darwinism for Christian belief. At this point, I want to introduce two other considerations. These are not "arguments," but are rather historical observations which raise further doubts concerning whether Dawkins has adequately justified his atheist reading of Darwinism. In what follows, we shall reflect on Darwin's own assessment of the religious implications of his theory of evolution, and the judgments of leading Christian biologists and theologians around the time of Darwin.

## The Religious Views of Charles Darwin

The religious implications of a Darwinian view of life are contested. It can be interpreted in a Christian, agnostic, and atheist manner. But what about Darwin himself? What was his own understanding of the religious implications of his views? It would suit Dawkins' purposes admirably if Darwin could be shown to have abandoned any faith in God as a consequence of his theory of evolution. Yet Dawkins' discussion of the complex and fascinating interaction of Darwin's scientific and religious views is most disappointing, and fails to deal satisfactorily with the issues involved.[40] If everything altered after Darwin, it is clearly important to determine what Darwin himself believed to have changed as a result of his new ideas.

The view that Darwin was indeed an atheist on account of his evolutionary doctrine was vigorously advocated in Edward Aveling's pamphlet *The Religious Views of Charles Darwin* (1883).[41] The evidence brought forward in this short work is far from persuasive, and it is unclear what weight should be attached to it. Darwin had earlier declined Aveling's request to dedicate his *Student's Darwin* to him. Aveson was one of Karl Marx's most dedicated English followers, and regarded Darwin's evolutionary views as reinforcing the basic ideas of

Marxian materialism. Darwin did not wish to endorse such an association.[42]

There are indeed several important passages in Darwin's writings that can be interpreted to mean that Darwin ceased to believe in an orthodox Christian conception of God on account of his views on evolution. The problem is that there are other passages which variously point to Darwin maintaining a religious belief, or to his losing his faith for reasons quite other than evolutionary concerns. However, a note of caution must be injected: on the basis of the published evidence at our disposal, it is clear that Darwin himself was far from consistent in the matter of his religious views. It would therefore be extremely unwise to draw any confident conclusions on these issues.[43]

There can be no doubt that Darwin abandoned what we might call "conventional Christian beliefs" at some point in the 1840s, although the dating of this must remain elusive. Yet there is a substantial theoretical gap between "abandoning orthodox Christian faith" and "becoming an atheist." Christianity involves a highly specific conception of God; it is perfectly possible to believe in a god other than that of Christianity, or to believe in God and reject certain other aspects of the Christian faith. Indeed, the "Victorian crisis of faith" – within which Darwin was both spectator and participant – can be understood as a shift away from the specifics of Christianity towards a more generic concept of God, largely determined by the ethical values of the day.

As any reasonable history of atheism makes clear, the alternatives available to the eighteenth and nineteenth centuries included many forms of belief in God, stretching far beyond the Christian vision of God. Voltaire (1694–1778), often thought of as an atheist, was in fact a Deist – one who believed in a divinity of reason. His *Letter to Uranie* (1722; published 1732) set out a strong defense of the existence of a supreme being, who was inadequately and falsely represented by the great positive religions of the world, especially the French Catholic Church and its leading representatives. Voltaire rejected the Christian concept of God on the grounds that it represented a distortion of the rival divinity of reason. There is a spectrum of theistic possibilities between "orthodox Christianity" and "atheism"; the later Darwin, as far as can be established, is to be located towards the middle of that spectrum, rather than at either of its extremes.

Two factors are known to have been a particular concern for Darwin, with negative implications for traditional Christianity. First, Darwin found the existence of pain and suffering in the world to be an unbearable intellectual and moral burden. It is widely agreed that what C. S. Lewis termed "the problem of pain" is one of the most significant obstacles to Christian belief, and it is entirely understandable that one as sensitive as Darwin should feel the weight of this matter, particularly in the light of his own protracted (and still unexplained) illness.[44] The death of his daughter Annie at the tender age of ten unquestionably deepened his feeling of moral outrage over this issue.[45]

In 1961 Donald Fleming put forward the important thesis that Darwin's experience of suffering was an integral element of his own loss of faith. Fleming held that Darwin came to believe that "modern man would rather have senseless suffering than suffering warranted to be intelligible because willed from on high."[46] Pain and suffering were to be accepted as the meaningless outcome of the evolutionary process; this, however disagreeable, seemed preferable to the alternative – namely, that God either inflicted suffering himself, or permitted it to be inflicted by others.

The idea that evolution took place according to certain general principles or laws, with the precise details left to chance, never entirely satisfied Darwin, seeming to leave many intellectual loose ends and open up difficult moral issues – not least, the immense wastage of life attending the process of natural selection. But it seemed to Darwin to be less troubling than the alternative – that "a beneficent and omnipotent God would have designedly created the Ichneumonidae with the express intention of their feeding within the living bodies of caterpillars."[47] At least this could be put down to an accident of nature, rather than purposeful divine design.

Second, Darwin shared the moral outrage of the mid-Victorian period over some aspects of Christian doctrine especially associated with the increasingly influential evangelical movement. Like George Eliot and many others at the time,[48] Darwin reacted with repugnance to ideas such as the damnation to everlasting Hell of those who did not explicitly believe the Christian gospel.[49] Darwin felt this outrage with particular force, on account of his father's somewhat unorthodox religious beliefs. As he wrote in his *Autobiography*:

I can indeed hardly see how anyone ought to wish Christianity to be true; for if so the plain language of the text seems to show that the men who do not believe, and this would include my Father, Brother and almost all of my friends, will be everlastingly punished. And this is a damnable doctrine.

In October 1882, six months after Darwin's death, his widow asked that this particular passage should not be published. She wrote the following in the margins of her husband's manuscript at this point:

I should dislike the passage in brackets to be published. It seems to me raw. Nothing can be said too severe upon the doctrine of everlasting punishment for disbelief – but very few now wd. call that "Christianity."

We can see here something of the spirit of this remarkable period in English cultural history, in which some aspects of evangelical Christianity were subjected to an unprecedented level of criticism, reflecting a growing belief that these accounts of the nature and purposes of God were deficient and unacceptable within an increasingly sophisticated culture.[50] Darwin here speaks with the voice of his age, and does not add anything of a specifically evolutionary character.

Darwin may have abandoned a traditional rendering of Christianity. However, this does not for one moment mean that he became an atheist. Although atheism is certainly encountered in late Victorian England, by far the more common response was agnosticism – a principled refusal to reach a decision on the God question, on the grounds of inadequate evidence.[51] Thomas H. Huxley, who invented the term, was profoundly irritated by those who dogmatized on matters of religion, whether positively or negatively. Science is, by definition, agnostic on matters of religion. And there, he argued, things should be left.

There is little in Darwin's writings to force us to any alternative conclusion. In 1879, while working on his autobiography, Darwin commented on his personal religious confusion: "My judgment *often fluctuates* . . . In my most extreme fluctuations I have never been an Atheist in the sense of denying God. I think that generally (and more and more as I grow older), *but not always*, that an Agnostic would be the more correct description of my state of mind."

Thus Darwin; but what of those who encountered Darwin's ideas at the time of their publication? What was the response to Darwin's new theory within the Victorian literary and religious establishment? As this reaction is rather illuminating, we may consider it in the final section of this chapter.

## The Christian Reaction to Darwin

Within thirty years of the publication of Darwin's *Origin of Species*, many within the establishment of the Church of England had swung behind the new ideas, and pronounced them to be perfectly consistent with Christian theology. This positive new attitude within the established church was noticed by most, including Huxley. In November 1887 he penned an essay in the journal *Nineteenth Century*, summarizing and evaluating three recent sermons by senior bishops of the Church of England. These were preac¹ ᴄd in Manchester Cathedral on Sunday, September 4, 1887, during the meeting of the British Association for the Advancement of Science, by the bishops of Carlisle, Bedford, and Manchester.[52] "These excellent discourses," Huxley wrote with evident enthusiasm, "signalize a new departure in the course adopted by theology towards science, and to indicate the possibility of bringing about an honourable *modus vivendi* between the two."

It is impossible to read the discourses of the three prelates without being impressed by the knowledge which they display, and by the spirit of equity, I might say of generosity, towards science which

76

pervades them. There is no trace of that tacit or open assumption that the rejection of theological dogmas, on scientific grounds, is due to moral perversity, which is the ordinary note of ecclesiastical homilies on this subject, and which makes them look so supremely silly to men whose lives have been spent in wrestling with these questions. There is no suggestion that an honest man may keep contradictory beliefs in separate pockets of his brain; no question that the method of scientific investigation is valid, whatever the results to which it may lead; and that the search after truth, and truth only, ennobles the searcher and leaves no doubt that his life, at any rate, is worth living.

Huxley welcomed this genuine attempt to achieve a rapprochement – no, more than that: a genuine convergence – of the natural sciences and theology. Perhaps his greatest enthusiasm was reserved for the firm rejection of any notion of demanding isolated intellectual compartments of the human mind for dealing with both. Huxley singled out one comment by the bishop of Bedford for especial praise, in which the bishop repudiated any idea that science and religion

occupy wholly different spheres, and need in no way intermeddle with each other. They revolve, as it were, in different planes, and so never meet. Thus we may pursue scientific studies with the utmost freedom and, at the same time, may pay the most reverent regard to theology, having no fears of collision, because allowing no points of contact.

Why bother with such historical details? Because they make it clear that it is deeply problematic to suggest that Darwinism *necessitates* atheism. As a matter of historical fact, Darwinism was not *perceived* to entail atheism by the best-informed judges of the time. Huxley's personal view was that it led to a principled agnosticism. However, his comments on these sermons indicates that he did not regard this as a completely closed question. While there was opposition, particularly from some popular preachers, to Darwin's ideas, the vast scholarly endeavor to understand both popular and academic reaction to them has demonstrated a far greater level of support for Darwin than was previously supposed.[53]

This support for Darwin was not restricted to the Church of England. A growing interest in Darwin is evident in North America around this time, even in those more conservative religious groups from which opposition might be expected. An excellent example of this positive assessment of Darwin can be found in Benjamin B. Warfield (1851–1921), widely regarded as the most important American theologian of the late nineteenth century. Although characterized by a conservative Protestant religious outlook, Warfield made clear his support for the concept of biological evolution.[54] Where Darwin regarded the evolutionary process as resting upon chance variations, whose subsequent fate was determined by general principles, Warfield argued it was entirely proper to see the evolutionary process as guided by divine providence.

In fact, the theory was widely accepted within early North American fundamentalism. The movement derives its name from a series of short publications entitled *The Fundamentals*, which appeared over the period 1912–17.[55] One of those fundamentalist essays was by James Orr, who argued evolution "is coming to be recognized as but a new name for 'creation,' only that the creative power now works from *within*, instead of, as in the old conception, in an *external*, plastic fashion."[56] Although hostile to Darwin's notion of random variations, Orr was clear that the process of natural selection could easily be viewed in terms consistent with Christian theism.

We might also pause here to note the views of Sir Ronald Fisher (1890–1962), one of the most important evolutionary biologists of the twentieth century.[57] Fisher, whose many theoretical achievements are noted by Dawkins, is often cited as the father of the neo-Darwinian synthesis. He was appointed Arthur Balfour Professor of Genetics at the University of Cambridge in 1943, and remained in that position until his retirement in 1957. He was awarded the Darwin Medal of the Royal Society in 1948 "in recognition of his distinguished contributions to the theory of natural selection, the concept of its gene complex and the evolution of dominance." Although a rather private man, Fisher was perfectly prepared to get involved in controversy whenever he believed scientific truth was being compromised. That he did not regard neo-Darwinism as entailing atheism

Plate 9    Ronald A. Fisher (1890–1962) © Science Photo Library

(or even agnosticism) is perfectly clear from a broadcast talk he gave on the BBC Third Programme in June 1947:

To the traditionally religious man, the essential novelty introduced by the theory of the evolution of organic life, is that creation was not all finished a long while ago, but is still in progress, in the midst of its incredible duration. In the language of Genesis we are living in the sixth day, probably rather early in the morning, and the Divine Artist has not yet stood back from his work, and declared it to be "very good." Perhaps that can only be when God's very imperfect image has become more competent to manage the affairs of the planet of which he is in control.[58]

Fisher retired to Australia in 1959, and is buried in Adelaide Cathedral, South Australia.

Stephen Jay Gould rightly pointed out that many leading Darwinians self-defined religiously, and saw no problem about doing so.[59] As Gould observes, any suggestion that Darwinian theory of evolution is *necessarily* atheistic goes way beyond the competency of the natural sciences, and strays into territory where the scientific method cannot be applied. If it is applied, it is *mis*applied. Thus Gould argues that Charles Darwin was agnostic (having lost his religious beliefs upon the tragic death of his favorite daughter), whereas the great American botanist Asa Gray, who advocated natural selection and wrote a book entitled *Darwiniana*, was a devout Christian.

More recently, Gould continues, Charles D. Walcott, the discoverer of the Burgess Shale fossils, was a convinced Darwinian and an equally firm Christian, who believed that God had ordained natural selection to construct a history of life according to His plans and purposes. More recently still, the "two greatest evolutionists of our generation" show radically different attitudes to the existence of God: G. G. Simpson was a humanist agnostic, Theodosius Dobzhansky a believing Russian Orthodox. As Gould concludes:

Either half my colleagues are enormously stupid, or else the science of Darwinism is fully compatible with conventional religious beliefs – and equally compatible with atheism.

And that, in a nutshell, seems to be where the debate has ended. Darwinism can be held to be consistent with conventional religious beliefs, agnosticism, and atheism. It all depends on how these terms are defined. The debate itself is fascinating, and opens up many important questions about the limits of the scientific method, the interpretation of the Bible, the evidential basis of faith, the transition from scientific theories to worldviews, and the history of biology. It is impossible to study, or become involved in, such debates without being challenged and stimulated to think through some of life's great issues.

But the debate, though immensely worthwhile and intellectually fascinating, is religiously inconclusive. Dawkins presents Darwinism as an intellectual superhighway to atheism. In reality, the intellectual trajectory mapped out by Dawkins seems to get stuck in a rut at agnosticism. And having stalled, it stays there. There is a substantial logical gap between Darwinism and atheism, which Dawkins seems to prefer to bridge by rhetoric, rather than evidence. If firm conclusions are to be reached, they must be reached on other grounds. And those who earnestly tell us otherwise have some explaining to do.

This neatly leads us on to consider the place of evidence in science and religion, an issue on which Dawkins has much to say.

# Proof and Faith:
# The Place of Evidence
# in Science and Religion

One of the central themes of the human quest for knowledge is the need to be able to distinguish mere "opinion" from "knowledge." How can we distinguish a belief that is warranted and rigorously reasoned from mere unsubstantiated opinion? The debate goes back to Plato, and continues today. The key question – whether in the natural sciences, philosophy, or theology – is this: what conditions must be fulfilled before we can conclude that a given belief is justified? For Dawkins, the only reliable knowledge we may hope to have of the world is scientific. Philosophers, lawyers, theologians, and others may make spurious claims to secure knowledge. In the end, however, it is only the natural sciences that can provide a true understanding of the world.

There is no doubt that the debate over how we generate and justify our beliefs is immensely important, and Dawkins' contribution to this debate must be welcomed, and – along with its rivals – taken seriously. In recent years, considerable attention has been paid to the way in which people sustain their belief systems. The evidence is disturbing, especially for those who continue to believe in the Enlightenment vision of complete objectivity of judgment in all things. Yet there is a growing body of evidence that belief systems – whether theistic or atheistic – are neither generated nor sustained in this way.

Cognitive psychological research has demonstrated repeatedly that people "tend to seek out, recall, and interpret evidence in a manner that sustains beliefs."[1] The interpretation of data is often deeply shaped by the beliefs of the researcher. These implicit beliefs are often so deeply held that they affect the way in which people process information and arrive at judgments. Both religious and anti-religious belief systems are often resistant to anything that threatens to undermine, challenge, qualify, or disconfirm them. Deeply held assumptions often render these implicit theories "almost impervious to data."[2]

Some Christian and Islamic writers seem unwilling to examine their deeply held beliefs, presumably because they are afraid that this kind of thing is bad news for faith. Well, maybe it is – for intellectually deficient and half-baked ideas. But it doesn't need to be like this. There are intellectually robust forms of faith – the kind of thing we find in writers such as Augustine of Hippo, Thomas Aquinas, and C. S. Lewis. They weren't afraid to think about their faith, and ask hard questions about its evidential basis, its internal consistency, or the adequacy of its theories.

Yet the problem is not limited to those who believe in God. As I discovered while researching my book *The Twilight of Atheism*, an atheist worldview can be just as detached from empirical evidence as a religious one. Dawkins has his own views of what religious people believe, and proceeds to rubbish these ideas with enthusiasm. Anyone who was theologically illiterate would doubtless be impressed by such a performance, and come to the conclusion that religion had been judged and found wanting at the most profound level. Well, it has certainly been judged. But whether that judgment can be sustained on the basis of the evidence is quite another matter.

To put it bluntly, Dawkins' engagement with theology is superficial and inaccurate, often amounting to little more than cheap point scoring. My Oxford colleague Keith Ward has made this point repeatedly, noting in particular Dawkins' "systematic mockery and demonizing of competing views, which are always presented in the most naive light."[3] His tendency to misrepresent the views of his opponents is the least attractive aspect of his writings. It simply reinforces the perception that he inhabits a hermetically sealed conceptual world, impervious to a genuine engagement with religion. Dawkins tends to seek out, recall, and interpret evidence in a manner that sustains his atheist beliefs. To illustrate this, we may open our discussion of the place of evidence in Dawkins' take on reality by exploring his approach to the idea of "faith."

## Faith as Blind Trust?

Faith "means blind trust, in the absence of evidence, even in the teeth of evidence."[4] This view, set out for the first time in 1976, is an expression of one of the "core beliefs" that determine Dawkins' attitude to religion. In 1989 he hardened his views: faith now qualified "as a kind of mental illness."[5] This non-negotiable core conviction surfaces again in 1992, when Dawkins delivered a lecture at the Edinburgh International Science Festival, in which he set out his views on the relation of faith and evidence. Dawkins was scathing over the intellectual irresponsibility of faith:

Faith is the great cop-out, the great excuse to evade the need to think and evaluate evidence. Faith is belief in spite of, even perhaps because of, the lack of evidence . . . Faith is not allowed to justify itself by argument.[6]

Four years later, Dawkins was named "Humanist of the Year." In his acceptance speech, published the following year in the journal *The Humanist*, Dawkins set out his agenda for the eradication of what he regarded as the greatest evil of our age.

It is fashionable to wax apocalyptic about the threat to humanity posed by the AIDS virus, "mad cow" disease, and many others, but I think a case can be made that *faith* is one of the world's great evils, comparable to the smallpox virus but harder to eradicate. Faith, being belief that isn't based on evidence, is the principal vice of any religion.

This is to be contrasted with the natural sciences, which offer an evidence-based approach to the world. "As a lover of truth, I am suspicious of strongly held beliefs that are unsupported by evidence."[7] And quite rightly so. But does this suspicion extend to his own strongly held atheist views, which to his critics seem surprisingly unsupported by the evidence he adduces?

Dawkins here opens up the whole question of the place of proof, evidence, and faith in both science and religion. It is a fascinating topic, and we must be grateful to him for so doing. In this chapter, we shall explore some of the issues raised by the history and philosophy of science for this debate, and ask if it really is quite as simple as Dawkins suggests. I certainly thought so during my atheist phase, and would have regarded Dawkins' arguments as decisive. But not now.

Let's begin by looking at that definition of faith, and ask where it comes from. Faith "means blind trust, in the absence of evidence, even in the teeth of evidence." But why should anyone accept this ludicrous definition? In his "Prayer for my Daughter" Dawkins makes an important point, which is clearly relevant here:

Next time somebody tells you that something is true, why not say to them: "What kind of evidence is there for that?" And if they can't give you a good answer, I hope you'll think very carefully before you believe a word they say.[8]

So what is the evidence that anyone – let alone religious people – defines "faith" in this absurd way?

The simple fact is that Dawkins offers no defense of this definition, which bears little relation to any religious (or any other) sense of the word. No evidence is offered that it is representative of religious opinion. No authority is cited in its support. I don't accept this idea of faith, and I have yet to meet a theologian who takes it seriously. It cannot be defended from any official declaration of faith from any Christian denomination. It is Dawkins' own definition, constructed with his own agenda in mind, being represented as if it were characteristic of those he wishes to criticize.

What is really worrying is that Dawkins genuinely seems to believe that faith actually is "blind trust," despite the fact that no major Christian writer adopts such a definition. This is a core belief for Dawkins, which determines more or less every aspect of his attitude to religion and religious people. Yet core beliefs often need to be challenged. For, as Dawkins once remarked of Paley's ideas on design, this belief is "gloriously and utterly wrong."

Faith, Dawkins tells us, "means blind trust, in the absence of evidence, even in the teeth of evidence." This may be what Dawkins thinks; it is not what Christians think. Let me provide a definition of faith offered by W. H. Griffith-Thomas (1861–1924), a noted Anglican theologian who was one of my predecessors as Principal of Wycliffe Hall, Oxford. The definition of faith that he offers is typical of any Christian writer:

[Faith] affects the whole of man's nature. It commences with the conviction of the mind based on adequate evidence; it continues in the confidence of the heart or emotions based on conviction, and it is crowned in the consent of the will, by means of which the conviction and confidence are expressed in conduct.[9]

It's a good and reliable definition, synthesizing the core elements of the characteristic Christian understanding of faith. And this faith "commences with the conviction of the mind based on adequate evidence." I see no point in wearying readers with other quotations from Christian writers down the ages in support of this point. In any case, it is Dawkins' responsibility to demonstrate that his skewed and nonsensical definition of "faith" is characteristic of Christianity through evidence-based argument.

Having set up his straw man, Dawkins knocks it down. It is not an unduly difficult or demanding intellectual feat. Faith is infantile, we are told – just fine for cramming into the minds of impressionable young children, but outrageously immoral and intellectually risible in the case of adults. We've grown up now, and need to move on. Why should we believe things that can't be scientifically proved? Faith in God, Dawkins argues, is just like believing in Santa Claus and the Tooth Fairy. When you grow up, you grow out of it.

This is a schoolboy argument that has accidentally found its way into a grown-up discussion. It is as amateurish as it is unconvincing. There is no serious empirical evidence that people regard God, Santa Claus, and the Tooth Fairy as being in the same category. I stopped believing in Santa Claus and the Tooth Fairy when I was about six years old. After being an atheist for some years, I discovered God when I was eighteen, and have never regarded this as some kind of infantile regression. As I noticed while researching *The Twilight of Atheism*, a large number of people come to believe in God in later life – when they are "grown up." I have yet to meet anyone who came to believe in Santa Claus or the Tooth Fairy late in life.

If Dawkins' rather simplistic argument has any plausibility, it requires a real analogy between God and Santa Claus to exist – which it clearly does not. Everyone knows that people do not regard belief in God as belonging to the same category as these childish beliefs. Dawkins, of course, argues that they both represent belief in non-existent entities. But this represents a very elementary confusion over which is the conclusion and which the presupposition of an argument.

In any case, Santa Claus and the Tooth Fairy are not ideas invented by children; these myths are forced upon them by adults, even if the children themselves often collude with them. Dawkins takes the view that belief in God is something forced upon children by tyrannical adults, and is to be rejected for that reason. Yet it is impossible to study the development of atheism in the twentieth century without noting how precisely this pattern of the imposition of ideas was found in the Soviet Union and other atheist states.[10]

In July 1954 the Communist Party of the Soviet Union ordered an increased explicit commitment to atheism in its schools. Belief in God had not yet been eliminated by argument or force. The only option seemed to be an aggressive program of indoctrination of its children. Soviet schoolbooks repeatedly asserted the malevolence of religion through slogans such as "Religion is a fanatic and perverse reflection of the world" or "Religion has become the medium for the spiritual enslavement of the masses." Alarmed at the persistence of religion, the Party decreed that "the teaching of school subjects (history, literature, natural sciences, physics, chemistry, etc.) should be saturated with atheism." In the end, all that the program did was to lay the foundations for the massive rebirth of belief in God after the collapse of the Soviet Union in the 1990s.

So, if Dawkins' argument carries weight, are we to conclude that atheism is evil, immoral, and incredible – the sort of nonsense that one has to force on children, because otherwise they would never believe it? No. The institutional abuse of an idea does not discredit it, whether we are talking about atheism, theism, or democracy. Yet this is such an obvious counter-argument that I am astonished that Dawkins does not even bother to note it. While I believe that it is wrong to force beliefs on children – whether theistic *or* atheistic – this does not invalidate those beliefs. It is merely the starting point for an argument, not its conclusion.

At times, Dawkins seems to get carried away with his anti-religious rhetoric by sliding from "this cannot be proved" to "this is false" with alarming ease, apparently unaware of the lapses in reasoning along the way. Consider, for example, his response in a 1999 debate on "Whether Science is Killing the Soul" to a question from the audience: can science offer consolation in the way that religion does – for example, after the death of a close friend or relative?

The fact that religion may console you doesn't of course make it true. It's a moot point whether one wishes to be consoled by a falsehood.[11]

Dawkins slides effortlessly from "consolation does not make religion true" to "religion is false." Now perhaps this is an entirely natural inference for Dawkins himself, given his deeply ingrained anti-religious feelings. But it is not a logically valid conclusion. It is clearly an obvious conclusion for Dawkins himself, steeped in a particular way of thinking driven by his core convictions. But it most certainly does not follow that, since *A* has not been proven, *A* is false.

As the core belief that faith is "blind trust" permeates Dawkins' many criticisms of religion, it clearly needs careful examination. Let's examine one of his statements on the nature of faith in a little more detail. In the second edition of *The*

*Selfish Gene,* Dawkins proposes an absolute dichotomy between "blind faith" and "overwhelming, publicly available evidence":

But what, after all, is faith? It is a state of mind that leads people to believe something – it doesn't matter what – in the total absence of supporting evidence. If there were good supporting evidence, then faith would be superfluous, for the evidence would compel us to believe it anyway.[12]

This, I must stress, is Dawkins' definition of faith, and it bears no resemblance to what Christians believe. It's on the same level as saying that the theory of evolution is about giraffes wanting to reach the leafy higher branches of trees, so that their necks stretch as a result. It's an amusing caricature of the real thing.[13] Sadly, some people take it seriously, and think it is the real thing.

Dawkins' idiosyncratic definition of faith is unworkable and unsustainable. It proposes an absolute dichotomy between "blind faith" and a belief grounded in "overwhelming, publicly available evidence." It's an interesting distinction, but it bears no relation to Christianity or to the normal working methods and assumptions of the natural sciences, including evolutionary biology. The issue is about probability, not certainty. The point at issue is that observational evidence can never render a prediction or generalization *certain*; it can, however, render either or both *probable*. The question is: *how* probable?

The highly simplistic model proposed by Dawkins seems to recognize only two options: 0 percent probability (blind faith) and 100 percent probability (belief caused by overwhelming evidence). Yet the vast majority of scientific information needs to be discussed in terms of the probability of conclusions reached on the basis of the available evidence. Some have argued for assessing the reliability of probability of a hypothesis on the basis of Bayes' theorem.[14] Such approaches are widely used in evolutionary biology. For example, Elliott Sober proposed the notion of "modus Darwin" for arguing for common Darwinian ancestry on the basis of present similarities between species.[15] The approach can only work on the basis of probability, leading to probabilistic judgments. But there's no problem here. It's an attempt to quantify the reliability of inferences.

And this applies as much to God, as to anything else. Dawkins asserts – for he certainly has not argued – that God is a matter of blind faith. He ended his 1992 lecture at the Edinburgh International Science Festival with the following dismissal of the God hypothesis. As Darwinism can explain the "spectacular beauty and complexity of life," there is no need for alternative or supplementary explanations:

The alternative hypothesis, that it was all started by a supernatural creator, is not only superfluous, it is also highly improbable. It falls foul of the very argument that was originally put forward in its favor. This is because any God worthy of the name must have been a being of colossal intelligence, a supermind, an entity of extremely low probability – a very improbable being indeed. Even if the postulation of such an entity explained anything (and we don't need it to), it still wouldn't help because it raises a bigger mystery than it solves.

Now this is not a reasoned argument. It is a hastily assembled garbled paragraph, jumbling together a number of ideas without the continuity of thought that distinguishes meandering sentences from trains of thought. But what is more worrying is the loose, imprecise, and vague talk about "improbability." God, we are told, is "highly improbable." Well, *how* improbable? And on what basis is this figure determined? Again, God is "an entity of extremely low probability." *How* low? And on the basis of what evidence is this probability determined? Just how does Dawkins arrive at any figure? And since when does probability determine whether or not something actually exists?

It is interesting to turn from this rather sloppy piece of rhetoric to a more careful argument by Richard Swinburne, Oxford University's Nolloth Professor of the Philosophy of Religion, who uses probability theory to assess the reliability of a belief in God – or, more specifically, the Christian belief that Jesus Christ is God incarnate.[16] I do not expect Dawkins to agree with Swinburne's theistic conclusion, or his calculation of the highly probable existence of God. But I do expect him to show the same careful attention to detail in assessing the relative probabilities of belief and unbelief, instead of his usual populist swashbuckling rhetorical exaggerations. After all, Dawkins, not Swinburne, is meant to be the scientist.

Dawkins concludes his 1992 lecture at the Edinburgh International Science Festival with these words: "We cannot prove that there is no God, but we can safely conclude that He is very, very improbable indeed." On the basis of the arguments offered, this is a highly unsafe conclusion, best passed over as an unscientific piece of rhetoric. Rather than dwell on this non-argument, let's turn to explore some more specific engagements with issues of faith. Let's ask a difficult, but obvious, question. Might atheism itself be a faith?

## Is Atheism Itself a Faith?

Is science a religion? Dawkins is often asked this question, and has a standard answer: No. The sciences, he argues, have all the good points of religious belief, and none of their bad points. They evoke a sense of wonder at reality, and offer humanity uplift and inspiration. And they are immune from the problems of faith. Atheism is the only option for today's thinking person, whose ideas are grounded in the only valid mode of encounter with reality – that of the natural sciences. It's a splendidly simple account of things.

It all starts to unravel very quickly, however. We have already noted Dawkins' belief that religious faith is "blind trust, in the absence of evidence, even in the teeth of evidence."[17] This arbitrary and idiosyncratic definition simply does not stand up to serious investigation. In fact, it is itself an excellent example of a belief tenaciously held and defended "in the absence of evidence, even in the teeth of evidence." Dawkins doggedly holds on to his own hopelessly muddled idea of what "faith" is, and assumes that others share that confusion. But what of atheism itself?

Dawkins presents agnosticism as an intellectual soft option, offering a rhetorical dismissal of the notion. In his Edinburgh Lecture of 1992 he argued that, like faith, agnosticism is a "cop-out" – an argument that can be applied to anything. "There is an infinite number of hypothetical beliefs we could hold which we can't positively disprove." Now there is unquestionably some truth in this. But the real difficulty is that Dawkins' biological arguments – to the extent that they *are* genuine arguments, rather than blunt dogmatic assertions – lead only to agnosticism. He is obliged to supplement them with additional arguments of a non-scientific nature to get to his intended conceptual destination. And these are often rhetorical, rather than analytical, in nature. In the end, Dawkins' atheism does not really rest on his science at all, but on an unstated and largely unexamined cluster of hidden non-scientific values and beliefs. As this point is so important, we shall explore it further.

The debate between atheism and religious belief has gone on for centuries, and just about every aspect of it has been explored to the point where even philosophers seem bored with it. The outcome is a stalemate. Nobody can prove God's existence, and nobody can disprove it. Dawkins, following G. G. Simpson, argues that everything changed with the publication of Darwin's *Origin of Species* in 1859.[18] So just what is the impact of Darwin on religious belief? That question has been explored in detail.

The basic conclusion, as we have seen, is that Darwinism neither proves nor disproves the existence of God (unless, of course, God is defined by his critics in precisely such a manner that his existence is defeated by some central presupposition of Darwinian theory). If the great debate about God were to be determined solely on Darwinian grounds, the outcome is agnosticism – a principled, scrupulous insistence that the evidence is insufficient to allow a safe verdict to be reached.

This does not suit Dawkins at all. His efforts to force an atheist conclusion upon a Darwinian description of the world are the least convincing, not to mention the least attractive, aspects of his writings. As an example, we may consider Dawkins' refutation of theism in *Climbing Mount Improbable*. Here, he argues that the very idea of a "designing God" is intellectually self-defeating:

Any designer capable of constructing the dazzling array of living things would have to be intelligent and complicated beyond all imagining. And complicated is just another word for improbable – and therefore demanding of explanation . . . Either your god is capable of designing worlds and doing all the other godlike things, in which case he *needs* an explanation in his own right. Or he is not, in which case he cannot *provide* an explanation.[19]

These are just assertions – bold, brash, confident statements, linked to the absolute dichotomist patterns of thought that Dawkins enjoys.

Let's begin with his first point about God being a "complicated" and hence "improbable" entity, on account of the richness of the biosphere. What does Dawkins mean when he makes the extraordinary statement that "any designer capable of constructing the dazzling array of living things would have to be intelligent and complicated beyond all imagining"? It's a bold assertion, made without the customary process of careful argument necessary to lead to such a conclusion, including the fair and thorough evaluation of alternative proposals.

It is far from clear what force this point has. Dawkins himself has devoted much of his career as a scientific popularizer to demonstrating that "the dazzling array of living things" could have arisen quite simply, over long periods of time, through a process of neo-Darwinian evolution. His point would have some merit as a critique of theism – though how much can be disputed – if he were to propose a doctrine of special, individual creation, similar to that proposed by William Paley. But there is no reason to do so. A theologian might respond by arguing that God created an environment within which incredibly complex entities could develop from quite simple beginnings by quite simple processes. Dawkins seems to think that believing in God commits one to this late eighteenth-century way of thinking about creation. But as the history of the Christian tradition up to, and since, that point makes clear, this is simply not the case.

Dawkins argues that, since God is "complicated," he is "improbable." These notions are not equivalent; nor is the latter entailed by the former. They are connected by a Kierkegaardian leap of faith, buttressed by an aggressive rhetoric rather than a rigorous, evidence-based argument. Yet, once more, it is quite unclear why this has any relevance. To reiterate the fundamental point made in the previous section: it does not matter whether God is improbable (setting to one side the fact that Dawkins neither quantifies this probability, nor offers us a method for determining that probability in the first place); improbable things happen. That, after all, is the point Dawkins makes in *Climbing Mount Improbable*. Improbabilities exist.

Anyway, why does God need to be *explained*? Which of the several diverging theories of scientific explanation is Dawkins basing this assertion upon? Carl Hempel's inferential model? Wesley Salmon's causal approach? Or one of the many other models which attempt to clarify whether an "explanation" actually explains *anything*? There is a singular lack of conceptual clarity in Dawkins' analysis, centering on the problematic yet critically important notion of explanation. As is well known, the philosophy of science has considered a variety of meaningful, yet quite different, concepts of scientific explanation,[20] none of which possess quite the reductive sense that Dawkins appears to presuppose. As Paul Kitcher points out, the most fundamental issue is the reduction of phenomena to as few "ultimates" as possible:

Science advances our understanding of nature by showing us how to derive descriptions of many phenomena, using the same pattern of derivation again and again, and in demonstrating this, it teaches us how to reduce the number of facts we have to accept as ultimate.[21]

So what's the problem with God, exactly? Why should God require an explanation at all? He might just be an "ultimate," to use Kitcher's term – one of those things we have to accept as given, and is thus amenable to description, rather than explanation. Dawkins needs to do a lot more work on what he means here before his point can be understood, and subjected to rigorous scrutiny.

One of the most striking things about Dawkins' atheism is the confidence with which he asserts its inevitability. It is a curious confidence, which seems curiously out of place

– perhaps even out of order – to those familiar with the philosophy of science. As Richard Feynman (1918–88), who won the Nobel Prize for physics in 1965 for his work on quantum electrodynamics, often pointed out, scientific knowledge is a body of statements of varying degrees of certainty – some most unsure, some nearly sure, but none absolutely certain.[22] Yet Dawkins seems to deduce atheism from the "book of nature" as if it were a pure matter of logic. Atheism is asserted as if it was the only conclusion possible from a series of axioms.

Many of a more philosophical inclination will want to ask a question at this point: given that the natural sciences proceed by inference from observational data, how can Dawkins be so sure about atheism? At times, he speaks with the conviction of a believer about the certainties of a godless world. It is as if atheism was the secure and inevitable result of a seamless logical argument. But how can he achieve such certainty, when the natural sciences are not deductive in their methods?

This difficulty has puzzled me throughout my reading of Dawkins' works. Inference is, by definition, an uncertain matter, in which one must take enormous trouble not to reach premature conclusions. So how come Dawkins is so sure about this? Others have examined the same evidence, and come to quite different conclusions. As will be clear from what has been said thus far, Dawkins' insistence that atheism is the only legitimate worldview for a natural scientist is an unsafe and unreliable judgment. Yet my anxiety is not limited to the flawed intellectual case that Dawkins makes for his convictions; I am troubled by the ferocity with which he asserts his atheism. One obvious potential answer is that the grounds of Dawkins' atheism lie elsewhere than his science, so that there is perhaps a strongly emotive aspect to his beliefs at this point. Yet I have not come across anything that forces me to this conclusion. The answer has to lie elsewhere.

I began to find an answer to my question while reading a careful analysis of the distinctive style of reasoning that we find in Dawkins' writings. In an important comparative study, Timothy Shanahan pointed out that Stephen Jay Gould's approach to the question of evolutionary progress was determined by an inductivist method, based primarily on empirical data.[23] Dawkins, he noted, "proceeded by elaborating the logic of 'adaptationist philosophy' for Darwinian reasoning." This being the case, Dawkins' conclusions are determined by a set of logical premises, which are ultimately – yet indirectly – grounded in the empirical data. "The very nature of a valid deductive argument is such that, given certain premises, a given conclusion follows of logical necessity quite irrespective of whether the premises used are true." In effect, Dawkins uses an essentially inductive approach to defend a Darwinian worldview – yet then extracts from this worldview a set of premises from which secure conclusions may be deduced.

Although Shanahan limits his analysis to exploring how Gould and Dawkins arrive at such antithetically opposed conclusions on the issue of evolutionary progress, his analysis is clearly capable of extension to Dawkins' religious views. Having inferred that Darwinism is the best explanation of observation, Dawkins proceeds to transmute a provisional theory into a certain worldview. Atheism is thus presented as the logical conclusion of a series of axiomatic premises, having the certainty of a deduced belief, even though its ultimate basis is actually inferential.

I have no doubt that Dawkins is persuaded of the case for atheism. Yet the case made is not *publicly* persuasive. Dawkins is obliged to make a "leap of faith" from agnosticism to atheism, corresponding to those who make a similar leap in the opposite direction. The idea that atheism is a form of faith is unproblematic. It amounts to little more than asserting what everyone knows to be true: that the things that really matter in life often lie beyond demonstrative proof. Nobody is going to be able to settle the question of the existence of God with complete certainty. It's simply not in the same category as whether the earth is flat, or whether DNA takes the form of a double helix. It's more like the question of whether democracy is better than totalitarianism. This cannot be settled by scientific means – but this does not prevent people from reaching their own conclusions on this matter. Nor does it entail that their decisions on such matters are irrational – a matter which we may explore a little further in the next section.

## Christian Faith as Irrational?

As we have seen, Dawkins' analysis of faith is highly simplistic, and takes no account of the way in which words are used in religious contexts. Ludwig Wittgenstein made the uncontestable point that words are used with different meanings in different contexts. For Wittgenstein, the *Lebensform* ("form of living") within which a word was used was of decisive importance in establishing its meaning. As Wittgenstein pointed out, precisely the same word can be used in a large number of contexts, with different meanings in each. One way of getting round this problem might be to invent a totally new vocabulary, in which the meaning of each word was tightly and unequivocally defined. But this is not a real option. Languages are living entities, and cannot be forced to behave in such an artificial way.

A perfectly acceptable approach, according to Wittgenstein, is to take trouble to define the particular sense in which a word should be understood, in order to avoid confusion with its many other senses. This involves a careful study of its associations and its use in the "form of living" to which it relates.[24] Instead of blindly and naively assuming that a word which means one thing in one situation means precisely the same in another, it is universally agreed that we need to take great care in establishing how words are used in each context, and the meanings that they bear.

This point ought to be familiar to any working scientist, who is perfectly used to using words in one sense in everyday life, and a more precise, restricted sense within a laboratory culture. I worked for several years during the late 1970s in Professor Sir George Radda's research group in Oxford University's department of biochemistry. Every weekday morning at 11.00, we gathered for communal coffee around an ancient gas ring. When someone asked a neighbor to "Pass the sugar!," what they were actually asking for was the chemical known as "sucrose" or, more precisely, [2-0-(alpha-D-glucopyranosyl)-beta-D-fructofuranoside]. Now in the natural sciences, the term "sugar" represents a very broad class of chemicals, which includes the specific sugars found in sugar cane (sucrose), milk (lactose), and various fruits (fructose). These vary greatly in "sweetness." Lactose, for example, has only 16 percent of the sweetness of sucrose.

The "sugar" of the everyday world is thus actually one very specific form of the more general scientific category of sugar – specifically, a 1,2'-glycoside. This simple difference of vocabulary can cause immense confusion, especially in relation to health problems arising from excessive sucrose consumption.[25] It might also have led to someone putting lactose in their coffee. We would have needed to pile six times the amount of lactose into our coffee to achieve the same degree of sweetness as sucrose. But this confusion just didn't arise. Everyone who gathered for coffee knew that words were being used with different meanings in different contexts, and could tell the difference between them.

Now there isn't a problem here. You just get used to living in different worlds, and sensitive to their subtle linguistic differences. You realize that words mean different things within different communities. Outsiders find these subtle differences troubling, and often fail to understand why the distinctive languages of different communities come into being. There is no question of dishonesty involved, as if anyone was trying to deceive people by using these specific forms of language. They evolve naturally, in response to the professional needs and distinctive tasks of the communities involved. It just involves becoming bilingual, and sensitive to the different meanings of words in different contexts. It means being prepared to ask people: "What do *you* mean when you use that word?" and being prepared to accept that *their* use of that word may not be identical with *your* use of the word – and that this doesn't mean that they are wrong, and you are right. Otherwise, communication across disciplinary boundaries becomes an impossibility. Scientists use language in a way that differs from ordinary usage; so do theologians. The first stage in any attempt to engage with a discipline is to understand its use of language.

Dawkins famously lambasted philosopher Mary Midgley for criticizing his "selfish gene" hypothesis without any awareness of how scientists used language. His words deserve to be cited:

[Midgley] seems not to understand biology or the way biologists use language. No doubt *my* ignorance would be just as obvious if I rushed headlong into *her* field of expertise, but I would then adopt a more diffident tone. As it is we are both in my corner, and it is hard for me not to regard the gloves as off.[26]

Yet is this the same Richard Dawkins who, knowing nothing about Christian theology, rushes headlong into the field, and tells theologians what they really mean when they use their own language? Or that they really mean "blind trust" when they speak of "faith"? There is a total failure on Dawkins' part to even begin to understand what Christian theology means by its language. It really does make it very difficult to take his judgments concerning its alleged failures with any degree of seriousness.

Let's try and get things straight here. As a professional historical theologian, I have no hesitation in asserting that the classic Christian tradition has always valued rationality, and does not hold that faith involves the complete abandonment of reason or believing in the teeth of the evidence. Indeed, the Christian tradition is so consistent on this matter that it is difficult to understand where Dawkins has got the idea of faith as "blind trust" from. Even a superficial reading of the works of leading Christian philosophers such as Richard Swinburne (Oxford University), Nicolas Wolterstorff (Yale University), and Alvin Plantinga (University of Notre Dame) would reveal their passionate commitment to the question of how one can make "warranted" or "coherent" statements concerning God.[27] There is no question of "blind trust." The issue is how one can make an informed, rational, and defensible judgment on the God question, when the evidence is so clearly ambivalent.

Now perhaps Dawkins is too busy writing books against religion to allow him time to read works of religion. On the rare occasions when he cites classic theologians, he tends to do so at second hand, often with alarming results. For example, Dawkins singles out the early Christian writer Tertullian (ca. 160–ca. 225) for particularly acerbic comment, on account of two quotations from his writings: "It is certain because it is impossible" and "it is by all means to be believed because it is

99

absurd."[28] Dawkins has little time for such nonsense. "That way madness lies."

In his view, Tertullian's approach – as evidenced by these two isolated citations – is just like that of the White Queen in Lewis Carroll's *Through the Looking-Glass*, who insisted on believing six impossible things before breakfast. As this dismissive account of Tertullian is one of the very few occasions on which Dawkins engages with serious representatives of the Christian theological tradition, I propose to take his comments with seriousness, and see where they take us. They might tell us something about Tertullian. Or even about Christianity. Or, then again, about Dawkins himself.

Tertullian never wrote the words "it is by all means to be believed because it is absurd." This misquotation is often attributed to him in secondary writings. But it is a misattribution, and has been known to be such for some time.[29] So at least we can reasonably assume that Dawkins has not read Tertullian himself, but has taken this citation from an unreliable secondary source. That might tell us something about how reliable his judgments are in these matters.

Tertullian did, however, write the words "it is certain because it is impossible." The context, however, makes it clear that he is not for one moment arguing for a "blind faith." Here is the full passage, in the original Latin, with my English translation:

Crucifixus est dei filius; non pudet, quia pudendum est.
Et mortuus est dei filius; credibile prorsus est, quia ineptum est.
Et sepultus resurrexit; certum est, quia impossibile.

The Son of God was crucified: I am not ashamed, because it is shameful.
The Son of God died: it is immediately credible, because it is clumsy.
He was buried, and rose again: it is certain, because it is impossible.[30]

In this passage, contrary to what Dawkins thinks, Tertullian is not discussing the relation of faith and reason, or the evidential basis of Christianity. Reading the passage in context immediately eliminates any such idea. It has been known since 1916 that Tertullian is playing around with some ideas from Aristotle in this passage. James Moffat, who pointed this out, notes the apparent absurdity of Tertullian's words:

This is one of the most defiant paradoxes in Tertullian, one of the quick, telling sentences in which he does not hesitate to wreck the sense of words in order to make his point. He deliberately exagger ates, in order to call attention to the truth he has to convey. The phrase is often misquoted, and more often it is supposed to crystallize an irrational prejudice in his mind, as if he scorned and spurned the intelligence in religion – a supposition which will not survive any first-hand acquaintance with the writings of the African father.[31]

The point being made is that the Christian gospel is profoundly counter-cultural and counter-intuitive at this point. So why would anyone want to make it up, when it is so obviously implausible, by those standards of wisdom? Tertullian then parodies a passage from Aristotle's *Rhetoric*, which argues that an extraordinary claim may well be true, precisely because it is so out of the ordinary. It was probably meant to be a rhetorical joke, for those who knew their Aristotle.

But this is only one of a whole series of arguments that Tertullian brings forward at this point, and it is grossly inac- curate to determine his entire attitude towards rationality on the basis of a single, isolated phrase.[32] Tertullian's attitude to reason is summed up definitively in the following quotation:

For reason is a property of God's, since there is nothing which God, the creator of all things, has not foreseen, arranged, and determined by reason. Furthermore, there is nothing God does not wish to be investigated and understood by reason.[33]

The bottom line is that there are no limits to what may be "investigated and understood by reason." The same God who created humanity with the capacity to reason expects that reason to be used in the exploration and representation of the world. And that's where the vast majority of Christian theolo- gians stand today, and have stood in the past. Sure, there are exceptions. But Dawkins seems to prefer to treat exceptions as if they were the rule, offering no evidence in support of this highly questionable conclusion.

Dawkins' views on the nature of faith are best regarded as an embarrassment to anyone concerned with scholarly accuracy. It does nothing for his credibility, especially his occasionally preachy statements like: "As a lover of truth, I am suspicious of strongly held beliefs that are unsupported by evidence."[34] So let's just draw a line under this nonsense, and pass on to something more interesting.

## The Problem of Radical Theory Change in Science

When I was learning physics at school, I gradually became aware of an awkward contradiction within what I was being taught. On the one hand, I was being assured that the theories of modern physics were completely reliable, the most secure form of knowledge that humanity could ever hope to possess. Yet every now and then, we would venture into a strange, twilight region, in which it would be explained to us, in hushed, conspiratorial tones, that "physicists once used to believe this, but don't now." Most of these had to do with light – something that was reasonably simple for a sixteen year old to understand. Once, it was thought that light required a medium to travel – but now, in the enlightened 1960s, nobody believed that any more. Once, people thought that light was made up purely of waves – but now we knew that it consists of photons. At first, I thought that these old-fashioned views dated back to the sixteenth century. But the awful truth soon became clear. The acceptance of these new ideas dated from about forty years earlier. "Once" turned out to mean "quite recently."

The problem of "radical theory change" in science cannot be overlooked in any responsible account of the scope of the scientific method. It is impossible to assume that today's scientific knowledge determines how things will be seen in future, or that today's scientific theories will continue to retain the confidence of future generations. There is no doubt that such confident attitudes were held in the late nineteenth century.[35]

Theoretical stability had been assumed to be a sign of theoretical truth. Yet this simply turned out to be complacency.

Many noted nineteenth-century scientists held that everything worth knowing was now known. In 1871 James Clerk Maxwell expressed his irritation with the idea that physics had uncovered all that could be known, so that all that remained was to establish measurements to the next place of decimals.[36] Max Planck relates how he found himself uncertain what subject to study at the University of Munich in 1875. His inclination to study the natural sciences was rubbished by the professor of physics at the university, who declared that nothing worthwhile remained to be discovered.[37] Robert A. Millikan – whose investigations of the electron broke new ground – recalls how physics was widely regarded as a "dead subject" in American academic circles during the early 1890s.[38] Such views were widespread, and can be found in many scientific writings of the period. The leading American astronomer Simon Newcomb felt able to assert in 1888 that more or less everything of importance had been seen and measured; what remained was to consolidate this body of knowledge.[39] Sure, a few more comets would be discovered. But the "big picture" was settled. It just remained for some more detail to be filled in.

The same was true in the field of evolutionary biology. Darwin's ideas rapidly became accepted as definitive, and inhibited further research in the field. This curious fact was pointed out by the geneticist William Bateson in 1909:

With the triumph of the evolutionary idea, curiosity as to the significance of specific differences was satisfied. The *Origin* was published in 1859. During the following decade, while the new views were on trial, the experimental breeders continued their work, but before 1870 the field was practically abandoned. In all that concerns the species the next thirty years are marked by the apathy characteristic of an age of faith. Evolution became the exercising-ground of essayists. The number indeed of naturalists increased tenfold, but their activities were directed elsewhere. Darwin's achievement so far exceeded anything that was thought possible before, that what should have been hailed as a long-expected beginning was taken for the completed work. I well remember receiving from one of the most earnest of my seniors the friendly warning that it was waste of time to study variation, for "Darwin had swept the field."[40]

From 1870 to 1900, such a degree of stability settled on the physical and biological sciences that many assumed that this temporary resting place was in fact the final destination.

By 1920, a revolution had taken place within physics. The great age of "classical physics" was over, and a new age dominated by quantum mechanics, the theory of relativity, and a "big bang" cosmology had dawned. There was no hint in the final decades of the nineteenth century of the tidal wave of change that was about to sweep over the natural sciences in the twentieth. Nobody in the nineteenth century seemed to have any idea of the massive upheavals that would take place, overturning many of the scientific certainties of the age. The theories seemed settled, assured, and constant. A century later, however, new theoretical "paradigms" – to use a term popularized by Thomas Kuhn[41] – had taken over.

Historians and philosophers of science have produced long lists of scientific theories, each of which was believed by one generation to be the best possible representation of reality, yet which were abandoned by later generations, in the light of new discoveries and increasingly precise measurements of what was already known. Some theories have proved remarkably stable; many have been radically modified, and others abandoned altogether.[42]

As Michael Polanyi (1891–1976), a chemist and noted philosopher of science, pointed out, natural scientists find themselves having to believe some things that they know will later be shown to be wrong – but not being sure *which* of their present beliefs would turn out to be erroneous. How can Dawkins be so sure that his current beliefs are true, when history shows a persistent pattern of abandoning of scientific theories as better approaches emerge? What historian of science can fail to note that what was once regarded as secure knowledge was eroded through the passage of time?

Scientific theorizing is thus *provisional*. In other words, it offers what is believed to be the best account of the experimental observations currently available. Radical theory change takes place either when it is believed that there is a better explanation of what is currently known, or when new information comes to light which forces us to see what is presently known in a new light. Unless we know the future, it is impossible to take an absolute position on the question of whether any given theory is "right." What can be said – and, indeed, must be said – is that this is believed to be the best explanation currently available. History simply makes fools of those who argue that every aspect of the current theoretical situation is true for all time. The problem is that we don't know which of today's theories will be discarded as interesting failures by future generations.

If theories are thus subject to erosion, what of worldviews that are based upon them? What happens to a worldview, if its theoretical foundations collapse? Once more, history provides us with ample warnings of what happens when a theory underpinning a worldview collapses. Like a house of cards, the worldview follows suit.

In the case of Darwinism, there is an additional difficulty. While Charles Darwin wanted to offer an explanation of how the present forms of animal and plant life emerged, he found that some of the pieces of evidence in that argument were historical. Any attempt to verify the Darwinian theory of evolution requires knowledge of the past. Yet can the scientific method actually be applied to the study of the past? The point is that such a method must use presently accessible evidence to reconstruct what happened in the past – but with what degree of plausibility?

So important was this difficulty that in 1976 Karl Popper expressed hesitation over whether the Darwinian theory of natural selection could strictly be said to fall within the scope of a scientific method, and hence be deemed "scientific" in character.[43] This is now seen as an over reaction based on a legitimate concern. There remains a significant degree of uncertainty and provisionality to any conclusions that are based on an analysis of the past, precisely because we cannot directly access the earth's past history. While this consideration is not sufficient to undermine Darwin's original theory, it does nevertheless raise concerns which cannot be ignored, and which must lead to a degree of modesty concerning whatever conclusions we draw from an analysis of the past.

All these concerns, taken together, raise a difficult question, which cannot be answered with any degree of certainty. Will the Darwinian theory of evolution itself one day have to be radically modified, or even abandoned, suffering the same fate as so many other scientific theories of the past? And what then becomes of the confident statements about the meaning of life made on its basis? Dawkins is aware of this problem, and is quite explicit about its consequences:

Darwin may be triumphant at the end of the twentieth century, but we must acknowledge the possibility that new facts may come to light which will force our successors of the twenty-first century to abandon Darwinism or modify it beyond recognition.[44]

Quite so.

While Dawkins is quick to rubbish those who suggest that faith plays a role in science, his arguments for doing so do not really meet the point at issue. The issue is not, as Dawkins seems to think, whether the natural sciences base their theories on blind instinct, rather than careful assessment of the available evidence. There is no doubting the critical, fundamental role of evidence-based reasoning in the sciences. Rather, the issue concerns the undeniable historical fact that the "available evidence" is situationally determined. The evidence available to future generations – for example, through technological advance – may force radical theoretical revision upon us.

There is therefore no contradiction in stating "it is believed that Darwinism is currently the best explanation of the development of biological life." This statement affirms that the evidence and theoretical models currently available are accepted as being the most robust and coherent, while allowing for future evidential and theoretical developments which may cause revision or eventual rejection of today's approaches.

The implications of this are perfectly clear, as are its religious and metaphysical implications. It is absolutely correct to say "evolutionary biologists currently believe that Darwinism is the best theoretical explanation of earth's life-forms." But this does not mean that future evolutionary biologists will share this judgment. We may *believe* that Darwinism is right, but we do not *know* that this is so. To do this, we need to stand in a hypothetical position, which allows us to see the evidence of the future. On the basis of what we currently know, we may hold this theoretical position; however, the history of science makes it clear that new evidence has a habit of arising, causing radical revision – perhaps even abandonment – of many long-held theories. Will Darwinism be one of them? And what then will happen to any worldviews, atheist or theist, which are founded on this same Darwinism? The only honest answer is that we don't know. Darwinism, like any other scientific theory, is best seen as a temporary resting place, not a final destination.

## The Rhetorical Amplification of the Case for Atheism

*Res ipsa loquitur* – "the thing speaks for itself." In the first period of my love affair with the natural sciences, I had what I now recognize to be completely unrealistic expectations of the discipline. One of these was the charmingly naive idea, capable of being entertained only by a idealist teenager, that the natural sciences were completely evidence-based, and demonstrated their conclusions only by an appeal to that evidence. Where other, lower, intellectual disciplines made use of verbal wheedling and other tricks of the persuader's trade, these were completely redundant in the sciences. Evidence, and evidence alone, was the sole determinant of truth. "Good research needs no rhetoric."

I still love the sciences. Yet it is now clear to me that some natural scientists use rhetoric beyond acceptable limits in pressing their case – often, it must be said, when venturing beyond their field of competence, or when attempting to cover up a deficit of experimental evidence with a verbal smokescreen. No wonder that cultural critics have started to read scientific journals and literature with a view to exposing some of the argumentative sleights of hand and hidden persuaders embedded in those texts.[45] And the level of rhetoric is a surefire indicator of the contentiousness of the argument. The greater the appeal to rhetoric, the weaker the argument.

What sort of techniques? One of the simplest rhetorical techniques is to associate your critics with whatever your intended readership regards as social outcasts. In the case of sociobiology – the scientific discipline widely seen as most rhetorically freighted – this means creating the impression that disagreement with them lumps you along with religious fundamentalists or science haters. The works of E. O. Wilson are often singled out for an excessive use of this kind of rhetoric. As Daniel Dennett points out, Wilson tends to portray his critics as nothing but "religious fanatics or scientifically illiterate mysterians." Anyone unwise enough to disagree with Wilson is likely to be pilloried as "a benighted, science-fearing skyhooker."[46] This isn't science, and everyone knows it.

Dawkins is fascinating to read with this point in mind. His wonderful way with words has often been noted, and I share in the general admiration for his lucidity of expression and superb illustration of often complex points, particularly in *The Selfish Gene* and *The Extended Phenotype*. This is Dawkins at his best – the effective scientific communicator. Yet one reads other works – particularly the ephemeral and somewhat lightweight essays collected together in *A Devil's Chaplain* – and forms a quite different impression. As Robert McFarlane pointed out in reviewing this work in the *Spectator*, Dawkins all too often "comes across as science's hired muscle: the bruiser in the bad suit with the baseball bat." In these essays, we find what is often a surprisingly shallow argument buttressed by a correspondingly aggressive prose.

After reading Dawkins' substantial output, I found that a rhetorical analysis of his works suggested that they could easily be divided into two categories.

1 The first consists of most of his published books, with the significant exceptions of *A Devil's Chaplain* and *Unweaving the Rainbow*. This category also includes some of his shorter academic works, particularly early papers dealing with ethological questions. In these works, we find a strongly

evidence-based mode of argument, with alternative view-points carefully and thoughtfully presented, and assessed in the light of the data. While Dawkins uses traditional rhetorical tools in these works, they are kept on a tight leash. Even if the reader disagrees with Dawkins' inter-pretation of evidence, the priority of detailed engagement with experimental findings as a shared defining assumption between author and reader is maintained.

2   The second consists mostly of shorter works, dealing with things that Dawkins does not like much – above all, religion. Here anecdote displaces evidence, and alternat-ives are generally rubbished. The tone of these writings is aggressive and dismissive, and shows little, if any, attempt to take alternatives seriously. They are often characterized by a strongly dichotomist mode of argument: "it is either *A* or *B*, and *B* is utterly stupid, so it must be *A*." The rhetorical index of these pieces is remarkably high – so high, in fact, that it is sometimes difficult to believe that this is the same evidence-responsive author of *The Selfish Gene*. Both *Unweaving the Rainbow* and the collection of papers gathered together as *A Devil's Chaplain* deploy an unusually large number of rhetorical devices, often in place of more rigorous argumentation. As one journalist percept-ively commented, "twin obsessions form virtually every piece [of *A Devil's Chaplain*] – Darwinian evolution (hurrah!) and religion (boo!)."[47]

Let's begin with one of Dawkins' most robustly scientific works, which is rigorously evidence-driven. I first read Dawkins' doctoral thesis on a cold winter's afternoon in Oxford Univer-sity's Radcliffe Science Library.[48] It is a fascinating piece of research, based on the meticulous observation of the behavior of domestic chicks when confronted with stimuli of various kinds. Dawkins approached his research with a range of poss-ible models of decision-making. At every point, the sovereignty of the empirical was affirmed. Every model proposed for how chicks decide whether to peck and what to peck was rigorously evaluated on the basis of carefully designed and controlled experiments. The behavior of a large number of chicks was carefully examined and compared critically with other published studies in the field (such as Impekhoven's famous studies of black-headed gull chicks). The thesis is a model of objective, detached, evidence-based scientific research.

When it comes to dealing with the behavior of religious people, Dawkins seems to step outside this rigorously empirical approach. The careful language, meticulous research, and rigorous standards of justification of the laboratory are swapped for those of the soapbox. In contrast to his ethological studies of chicks, Dawkins offers an "ethology of religious people" from which any detailed empirical analysis is wanting. Where one might hope to find reference to extensive systematic observation of the impact of religious behavior on people – there is a vast body of data – one finds instead flagrantly biased anecdotes and hopelessly unsubstantiated generalizations. Rhetoric displaces careful observation and analysis.

There is a large and growing literature dealing with the impact of religion – whether considered generically, or as a specific form of faith – upon individuals and communities.[49] Although it was once fashionable to suggest that religion was some kind of pathology,[50] this view is now retreating in face of mounting empirical evidence that suggests (but not conclusively) that many forms of religion might actually be beneficial.[51] Sure, some forms of religion can be pathological and destructive. Others, however, seem to be rather good for you.

A 2001 survey of 100 evidence-based studies to systematically examine the relationship between religion and human wellbeing disclosed the following:

- 79 reported at least one positive correlation between religious involvement and well-being.
- 13 found no meaningful association between religion and well-being.
- 7 found mixed or complex associations between religion and well-being.
- 1 found a negative association between religion and well-being.[52]

Dawkins' entire worldview depends upon precisely this negative association between religion and human well-being which only 1 percent of the experimental results would seem unequivocally to affirm, and 79 percent equally unequivocally to reject. The results make at least one thing abundantly clear: we need to approach this subject in the light of the scientific evidence, not personal prejudice.

For Dawkins, the issue is simple: the question is "whether you value health or truth."[53] As religion is false – one of the unassailable core beliefs which recurs throughout his writings – it would be immoral to believe, whatever benefits it might bring. Yet Dawkins' arguments that belief in God is false just don't add up. That's probably why he supplements them with the additional argument that religion is bad for you. The growing body of evidence that religion actually promotes human well-being is highly awkward for him here. Not only does it subvert a functional argument for atheism; it begins to raise some very troubling questions about its truth as well.

Although Dawkins himself is highly critical of "the superficial seductiveness of individual stories that seem – but only seem – to show a pattern,"[54] he nevertheless seems to rely excessively on precisely the patterns selectively disclosed by such individual stories in his routine rubbishing of religious people and ideas. His essay "Viruses of the Mind," from which this citation is taken, is an excellent example of the selective use of this device.[55]

One of this essay's central arguments is that religious people do some very bad things. In his jolly swashbuckling way, Dawkins piles up the anecdotes to tell us how awful religious people are. They believe utterly stupid, pedantic, and pointless things (like the doctrine of the Trinity), or fuss about trivia (such as nitpickingly precise kosher food laws). Intelligent people – such as the philosopher Anthony Kenny – give up on religion. Instead of tolerating "the obvious contradictions within Catholic belief," he went on instead to become "a highly respected scholar." And, to cap it all, religion encourages the murder of its opponents, and other outrageous behavior.

Well, some religious people do indeed behave in unacceptable ways. Let's be honest about this. But how many? Dawkins is somewhat coy about statistics and detailed analysis of the available evidence. We have already seen how he also shies away from probabilistic approaches to belief evaluation. At points in his works, Dawkins seems to get carried away with his rhetoric, implying that religious people are all deceived and deceiving. But this highly selective appeal to evidence and easy dismissal of alternatives isn't scientific. It isn't even scientific grandstanding. It's just grandstanding.

Let's turn to Freeman Dyson for illumination here. Dyson – Professor of Physics at the Institute for Advanced Studies, Princeton – is probably one of the twentieth century's most respected physicists. He sums up the situation with what seems to be admirable fairness. Some religious people do dreadful things; others do wonderful things:

We all know that religion has been historically, and still is today, a cause of great evil as well as great good in human affairs. We have seen terrible wars and terrible persecutions conducted in the name of religion. We have also seen large numbers of people inspired by religion to lives of heroic virtue, bringing education and medical care to the poor, helping to abolish slavery and spread peace among nations.[56]

It's not as neat as Dawkins' polemical pastiche, but it has the merit of doing something approaching justice to the facts.

Everyone would agree that some religious people do some very disturbing things. But the introduction of that little word "some" to Dawkins' argument immediately dilutes its impact. For it forces a series of critical questions. How many? Under what circumstances? How often? It also forces a comparative question: how many people with *anti-religious* views also do some very disturbing things? And once we start to ask that question, we move away from cheap and easy sniping at our intellectual opponents, and have to confront some dark and troubling aspects of human nature. Let's explore this one.

I used to be anti-religious. In my teens, I was quite convinced that religion was the enemy of humanity, for reasons very similar to those that Dawkins sets out in his popular writings. But not now. And one of the reasons is my dreadful discovery of the dark side of atheism. Let me explain. In my innocence, I assumed that atheism would spread through the sheer genius of its ideas, the compelling nature of its arguments, its liberation from the oppression of religion, and the dazzling brilliance of the world it commended. Who needed to be coerced into such beliefs, when they were so obviously right?

Now, things seem very different. Atheism is not "proved" in any sense by any science, evolutionary biology included. Dawkins thinks it is, but offers arguments which are far from compelling. And yes, atheism liberated people from religious oppression, especially in France in the 1780s. But when atheism ceased to be a private matter and became a state ideology, things suddenly became rather different. The liberator turned oppressor. To the surprise of some, religion became the new liberator from atheist oppression. Unsurprisingly, these developments tend to be airbrushed out of Dawkins' rather selective reading of history. But they need to be taken with immense seriousness if the full story is to be told.

The final opening of the Soviet archives in the 1990s led to revelations that ended any notion that atheism was quite as gracious, gentle, and generous a worldview as some of its more idealistic supporters believed. *The Black Book of Communism*, based on those archives,[57] created a sensation when first published in France in 1997, not least because it implied that French communism – still a potent force in national life – was irreducibly tainted with the crimes and excesses of Lenin and Stalin. Where, many of its irate readers asked, were the "Nuremberg Trials of Communism"? Communism was a "tragedy of planetary dimensions" with a grand total of victims variously estimated by contributors to the volume at between 85 million and 100 million – far in excess of the excesses committed under Nazism.

Now, one must be cautious about such statistics, and equally cautious about rushing to quick and easy conclusions on their basis. Yet the basic point cannot really be overlooked. One of the greatest ironies of the twentieth century is that many of the most deplorable acts of murder, intolerance, and repression were carried out by those who thought that religion was murderous, intolerant, and repressive – and thus sought to remove it from the face of the planet as a humanitarian act. Even his most uncritical readers should be left wondering why Dawkins has curiously failed to mention, let alone engage with, the blood-spattered trail of atheism in the twentieth century – one of the reasons, incidentally, that I eventually concluded that I could no longer be an atheist.

Now I could draw the conclusion, based on a few choice stories – such as that of one of the greatest charlatans of the twentieth century, Madalyn Murray O'Hair, founder of American Atheists Inc.[58] – and a highly selective reading of history, that atheists are all totally corrupt, violent, and depraved. Yet I cannot and will not, simply because the facts do not permit it. The truth, evident to anyone working in the field, is that some atheists are indeed very strange people – but that most are totally ordinary people, just wanting to get on with their lives, and not wanting to oppress, coerce, or murder anyone. Both religion and anti-religion are capable of inspiring great acts of goodness on the part of some, and acts of violence on the part of others.

The real issue – as Friedrich Nietzsche pointed out over a century ago – is that there seems to be something about human nature which makes our belief systems capable of inspiring both great acts of goodness and great acts of depravity. To illustrate this point, we may turn to a little-told anecdote about science, which shows how it, like all other areas of human activity, can be used for good or for evil.

While studying organic chemistry at Oxford in the early 1970s, I made extensive use of a massive work entitled *Advanced Organic Chemistry*.[59] It was written by a husband and wife team, and was invariably referred to as "Fieser & Fieser." It was my companion through many a long evening in the college library, as I tried to make sense of some of the experiments I was working on at the time. Louis and Mary Fieser were based at Harvard University, where they pioneered some highly important synthetic breakthroughs. These included Vitamin K-1, the human body's blood-clotting agent (a major development for hemophilia) and cortisone (an important anti-inflammatory agent). In recognition of this and other successes,

Harvard named a new laboratory after them: the Louis and Mary Fieser Laboratory for Undergraduate Organic Chemistry was opened in 1996. Fittingly, Mary Fieser herself dedicated the new building, before her death in 1997. On any showing, the Fiesers made landmark contributions to chemistry, and to the advancement of human medical care. Arguably, the new synthetic routes they pioneered saved tens of thousands of lives.

Louis Fieser also pioneered another development at Harvard, not mentioned by those with uncritically positive views of the sciences. Napalm was one of the US military's most important weapons during the Korean and Vietnam wars. Manufactured by the Dow Chemical Corporation, napalm was a quick and effective way of neutralizing troops hidden in foxholes or under the cover of the jungle. It worked by burning them alive, or depriving them of oxygen through conflagration of the environment. Back in 1942, the US military had realized that there was little point in using gasoline as an incendiary device for this purpose. It burned up too quickly. What they really needed was gasoline which had been modified to burn more slowly, at greater temperatures. It would stick to people. And they would not be able to stop the material burning. Dissolving rubber in gasoline was one option. But rubber was in short supply. A chemical alternative was needed.

A research contract went out to develop jellified gasoline. Du Pont and Standard Oil invested heavily in trying to get there first. But the race was won by a small team based at Harvard, headed up by none other than Louis Fieser. (Interestingly, Mary does not seem to have been involved in this inhumane project.) Although Fieser and his team initially had hopes that divinylacetylene would create a gel that was sufficiently viscous to adhere to human flesh, this line of research proved unproductive. Instead, they found that gasoline could be jellified if added to about one tenth its weight of a powder of aluminium napthenate (made from crude oil residues) and aluminium palmitate (made from coconut oil). The sources of the materials gave the substance its acronym – Napalm. The use of both black powder and phosphorus in the bomb's fuse ensured that the burning, exploding material could not be extinguished. The moment it was exposed to air, it would ignite.

115

Some 77 million pounds of Fieser's formula were made during World War II. And most of it was used against the Japanese.

During the night of March 9–10, 1945, 279 low-flying US B-29 Superfortress bombers dropped 1,667 tons of napalm on Tokyo. The resulting firestorm devastated a vast built-up area of mainly wooden constructions. It remains uncertain precisely how many were burned alive, how many injured, and how many made homeless. As many as 100,000 may have died during that night. But whatever the statistics, it was unquestionably one of the most destructive acts of World War II, exceeding the initial damage and carnage later caused by the first atomic bomb.

Fieser protested that he was not responsible for the way in which his invention was used by other people. He even found a use for the product which did not involve burning people or buildings – getting rid of the common garden weed crabgrass (*Digitaria ischaemum*), burning away its seeds while leaving good grass roots untouched. Nevertheless, it was pointed out that napalm was *designed* to incinerate people and buildings. As it happened, an "improved" version of napalm was developed after the war by Dow, consisting of 46 percent polystyrene, 33 percent gasoline, and 21 percent benzene. Fieser's original formula was now of purely historical interest. But his invention had burned alive men, women, and children on a horrific scale.

Now, what are we to conclude from this anecdote? That all scientists are necessarily evil? Or that science itself is malevolent? Doubtless there are some who would wish to draw this conclusion, most notably those who are alarmed at the role of science and scientists in weapons development – something that Dawkins rather glosses over, by the way – and might want to use this story and others like it in an attempt to destroy the public reputation of science and scientists. But this would be just as invalid as the equally flawed attempts to smear atheism or religion on account of the acts of some of their followers. If these were demonstrably *typical* or *characteristic* acts, it would be different. The real question here concerns what is normal and what is aberrant behavior. It may suit his polemical purposes to treat the pathological as characteristic, or the aberrant as normal. But whether Dawkins likes it or not, most atheists, Christians, and scientists are ordinary people, neither extraordinarily virtuous nor extraordinarily evil.

Religious belief sometimes leads to evil, directly or indirectly. But religion has no monopoly in this respect, as if it was distinguished as the sole area of human life and thought that was marred in this manner. Even science itself can be abused, as some of the more sinister medical developments in Nazi Germany made abundantly clear. Yet Dawkins would surely argue that this is an *abuse* of science, quite untypical of its normal values and approaches. And I would agree. Yet if this defensive strategy can be permitted for science, why not also for religion? Why not recognize what most people already know: that it is the *abuse* of religion that is pathological and destructive? Religion, like all other areas of human activity and thought, needs to be reformed, reviewed, and corrected – but not abolished.

There is a very serious issue here, which needs to be discussed openly and frankly by atheists, Christians, and scientists alike – namely, how some of those who are inspired and uplifted by a great vision of reality end up doing such dreadful things. This is a truth about human nature itself. If we are indeed to have an "open society," there needs to be a careful and informed discussion of how we are to avoid violence and aggression. And pretending that religion is the only problem in the world, or the base of all its pain and suffering, is no longer a real option for thinking people. It's just rhetoric, masking a difficult problem we all need to address – namely, how human beings can coexist and limit their passions.

So is religion "blind faith," which flies in the face of the evidence? Hardly. This definition is itself a piece of rhetoric, devised to meet the needs of Dawkins' agenda. When I debate these issues in public, I regularly get asked why Christians blindly trust in God, in the absence of any supporting evidence. I ask if they would be kind enough to tell me where they find such a ludicrous idea, and to justify it from a serious Christian writer of note. I am usually greeted with an embarrassed silence. Yet on occasion, I get the answer: "Well, that's what Richard Dawkins says." The audience usually laughs. They get the point.

Yet in his rather condescending "Prayer for My Daughter," Dawkins tells her that a "bad reason for believing anything" is "that you are told to believe it by somebody important."[60] So why should anyone believe Dawkins when he tells us what Christians believe faith to be? His idiosyncratic definition is his own invention, created, it would seem, for purely polemical purposes. It would be nice if we found evidence-based analysis brought to bear on the issue, so that the discussion was based on what Christians actually believe, rather than what Dawkins thinks we believe. Then we might actually get somewhere in a discussion about the relation of science and religion.

# Cultural Darwinism?
# The Curious "Science"
# of Memetics

Darwinism is too big a theory to be limited to the field of biology. Why restrict Darwinism to the world of the gene, when it is laden with significance for every aspect of human life and thought? In *The Selfish Gene* (1976), Dawkins explains that he had long been interested in the analogy between cultural and genetic information. Might not Darwinian theory be applied to human culture, as much as to the world of biology? This intellectual move lays the ground for converting Darwinism from a scientific theory to a worldview, a metanarrative, an overarching view of reality.

The move, however, requires a cultural equivalent to the gene – a "cultural replicator," which ensures the transmission of information across time and space. If this concept of a cultural replicator could be established on a firm scientific basis, Darwinism would be transformed into a universal method, reaching beyond the specific domain of biological evolution to include the world of culture.[1]

Dawkins stands in a long tradition of those who have attempted to apply the theory of evolution to human culture, including Herbert Spencer in the nineteenth century, and

E. O. Wilson in the twentieth. The evolutionary psychologist Donald T. Campbell (1916–96) developed the idea of a "cultural replicator" as early as 1960,[2] and introduced the term "mnemone."[3] The related idea of the "culturgen" has found particular acceptance within North American sociobiology.[4]

Although the notion of a cultural replicator is thus far from new, Dawkins has done much to popularize the concept, and make it accessible to a wider audience through his simple terminology and illustrations. Above all, he introduced the term which has come to dominate popular discussion of the issue – the "meme." In part, the greater success of this term can be put down to the neater and more memorable terminology Dawkins developed. Yet another factor was the greater popular reach of his writings, which allowed a much wider reading public to become aware of the potential of essentially biological analogues for cultural development. As a result, Dawkins' work has generated considerable popular discussion.[5]

In this chapter, we shall explore Dawkins' central contribution to a Darwinian account of the evolution of human culture – a specific conception of the cultural replicator, which he named the "meme." From the outset, Dawkins associated his idea of the "meme" with issues of religious belief, regarding religions as "the prime examples of memes."[6] Given this, it is clearly important to explore this concept in this work, and locate it within the broad spectrum of recent atheist critiques of religious beliefs.

A series of writers – including Karl Marx (1818–83) and Sigmund Freud (1856–1939) – argued that, since there is no God to believe in, human religious belief is essentially an invention designed to provide "metaphysical comfort" (Nietzsche) to an existentially beleaguered humanity.[7] Dawkins develops this approach in a new direction, arguing that religions are basically "mind parasites." Belief in God is to be seen as "self-replicating information" that "leaps infectiously from mind to mind." It is an idea that Dawkins finds both academically attractive and humanly repulsive,[8] and has come to feature prominently in recent popular atheist polemical writings. But is it right?

In what follows, I shall explore the origins of Dawkins' con-cept of the "meme," and address four critical difficulties that confront this specific idea, before moving on to consider Dawkins' later idea that God is a parasitic "virus of the mind." These difficulties may be summarized as follows.

- There is no reason to suppose that cultural evolution is Darwinian, or indeed that evolutionary biology has any particular value in accounting for the development of ideas.
- There is no direct evidence for the existence of "memes" themselves.
- The case for the existence of the "meme" rests on the questionable assumption of a direct analogy with the gene, which proves incapable of bearing the theoretical weight that is placed upon it.
- There is no necessary reason to propose the existence of a "meme" as an explanatory construct. The observational data can be accounted for perfectly well by other models and mechanisms.

We shall return to consider these in more detail, after we have explored how the notion of the "meme" arose.

## The Origins of the Meme

In an important article of 1968, expanded in 1975, the anthro-pologist F. T. Cloak proposed that culture evolved through an essentially Darwinian mechanism, and set out how ethological methods might be applied to culture-specific behavior.[9] The question of whether it is possible to identify and study cultural replicators, directly analogous to genes, had thus been raised before Dawkins published *The Selfish Gene*.

Cloak's model was clearly of importance to Dawkins as he wrote *The Selfish Gene*. Cloak drew a distinction between "i-culture" (the set of cultural instructions that are contained in the nervous system) and "m-culture" (relationships in material structures which are maintained by such instructions, or changes in material structures which come about as a result of these instructions).

Dawkins recalls how he wanted a word for a "cultural replicator" that sounded like "gene" – thus stressing the analogy between cultural and genetic transmission – and came up with "meme"[10] – an abbreviation of the term "mimeme," derived from the Greek *mimesis* ("imitation"). The meme was proposed as a hypothetical replicator – "a unit of cultural transmission, or a unit of *imitation*"[11] – to explain the process of the development of culture within a Darwinian framework:

Just as genes propagate themselves in the gene pool by leaping from body to body via sperm or eggs, so memes propagate themselves in the meme pool by leaping from brain to brain by a process which, in the broad sense of the term, can be called imitation.

As examples of what he has in mind, Dawkins points to such things as tunes, ideas, catch-phrases, fashions, aspects of architecture, songs – and God.

Yet there is a problem with this definition of the meme. In Dawkins' account of the neo-Darwinian synthesis, it is the *gene* that is the unit of selection, even though it is the *phenotype* which is actually subject to the process of selection. The gene is the replicator, or the set of instructions; the phenotype is the physical manifestation of the organism, the visible characteristics or behavior resulting from that set of instructions. Yet all the examples of "memes" that Dawkins offers in *The Selfish Gene* are the *result* of such instructions, not the instructions themselves.[12] While Dawkins proposed an analogy between *meme* and *gene*, he actually illustrated this by appealing to the cultural equivalent of *phenotypes*, not genes. Dawkins' suggestion of a parallel between the propagation of genes in the gene pool and memes in a (hypothetical) meme pool was thus not entirely warranted.

Dawkins recognized this problem, and modified his ideas in his next major popular work – *The Extended Phenotype* (1982). His original account of the meme, he conceded, was defective; it required correction.

I was insufficiently clear about the distinction between the meme itself, as replicator, and its "phenotypic effects" or "meme products" on the other. A meme should be regarded as a unit of information residing in a brain (Cloak's "i-culture"). It has a definite structure, realized in whatever medium the brain uses for storing information ... This is to distinguish it from phenotypic effects, which are its consequences in the outside world (Cloak's "m-culture").[13]

This clarification removed one fundamental difficulty with the concept of the meme. On any standard neo-Darwinian account, genes give rise to phenotypes. There is no question of phenotypical causation of genetic traits. To put it in a nutshell: genes are *selected, not instructed*.[14] Dawkins, who vigorously defends this "central dogma" of Darwinian orthodoxy, had put himself in a potentially indefensible position, in that he appeared to imply that it was phenotypes that were inherited.

This new definition of the meme identifies it as the fundamental unit of information or instruction which gives rise to cultural artifacts and ideas. It is the set of instructions, the blueprint, not the product. What Dawkins originally defined as memes – things like "catchy tunes" – are now to be regarded as "meme products." At a popular level, however, Dawkins' meme concept continues to be discussed in terms of his 1976 definition, set out in *The Selfish Gene*, rather than its 1982 revision, as presented in the somewhat less widely read *Extended Phenotype*.

So what is the relevance of this to God? Dawkins is an atheist, and incorrectly believes that religious faith is "blind trust," which refuses to take account of evidence. So why do people believe in God, when there is no God to believe in? Dawkins' answer lies in the ability of a God-meme to replicate itself in the human mind. The "god-meme" performs particularly well because it has "high survival value, or infective power, in the environment provided by human culture."[15] People do not believe in God because they have given long and careful thought to the matter; they do so because they have been infected by a powerful meme. (This idea would later be developed in terms of the imagery of God as a virus.) In both cases, the intent and outcome is a subversion of the intellectual legitimacy of belief in God. The God-meme or God-virus is just good at infecting people.

The same, of course, would also be true for an "atheism"-meme. Dawkins does not deal with how atheism spreads on the basis of his memetic approach, presumably on account of his core belief that atheism is scientifically correct. In fact, it is itself a belief, which requires explanation. Dawkins' model actually requires that both atheism and belief in God should be seen as memetic effects. They are therefore equally valid – or equally invalid, for that matter.

The problem with this approach is immediately obvious. If all ideas are memes, or the effects of memes,[16] Dawkins is left in the decidedly uncomfortable position of having to accept that his own ideas must also be recognized as the effects of memes. Scientific ideas would then become yet another example of memes replicating within the human mind. This would not suit Dawkins' purposes at all, and he excludes the notion in an intriguing manner:

Scientific ideas, like all memes, are subject to a kind of natural selection, and this might look superficially virus-like. But the selective forces that scrutinize scientific ideas are not arbitrary or capricious. They are exacting, well-honed rules, and they do not favor pointless self-serving behavior.[17]

This represents a case of special pleading, in which Dawkins makes an unsuccessful attempt to evade the trap of self-referentiality. Anyone familiar with intellectual history will spot the pattern immediately. Everyone's dogma is wrong except mine. My ideas are exempt from the general patterns I identify for other ideas, which allows me to explain them away, leaving my own to dominate the field.

But why on earth is conformity to scientific criteria allowed to determine whether a meme is "good" or "useful"? On any conventional reading of things, a "good" or "useful" meme would be one that promoted harmony, gave someone a sense of belonging, or increased life expectancy. These would seem far more natural and obvious criteria for "good" memes. But on further reflection, the truth dawns on us. There are no "natural" criteria involved at all. We decide whether we like them or not, and then label the memes accordingly. If you like religion, it's a "good" meme; if not, it's "bad." In the end, all that Dawkins does here is to construct an entirely circular argument, reflecting his own subjective system of values.

We shall return to explore the idea of "God as a virus" later in the present chapter. But first, we need to develop the four objections, noted earlier, which have led most to abandon the "meme" as a serious tool of scientific research. As Simon Conway Morris pointed out, memes seem to have no place in serious scientific reflection:

Memes are trivial, to be banished by simple mental exercises. In any wider context, they are hopelessly, if not hilariously, simplistic. To conjure up memes not only reveals a strange imprecision of thought, but, as Anthony O'Hear has remarked, if memes really existed they would ultimately deny the reality of reflective thought.[18]

## Is Cultural Development Darwinian?

My own interest in intellectual history developed at more or less the same time as Dawkins first set out the "meme" theory. When I first encountered the idea of the "meme" in 1977, I found it immensely exciting. Here was something which was potentially open to rigorous evidence-based investigation, offering new possibilities for the study of intellectual and cultural development. Why was I so optimistic about the idea? I was in the process of beginning what would be one of my lifetime concerns: the history of ideas. My particular interest lay in how religious ideas develop over time, and the factors that lead to their development, modification, acceptance or rejection, and – at least in some cases – their slow decline into oblivion.

The "meme," I thought at the time, would allow me to create and validate robust and reliable models for intellectual and cultural development, firmly grounded in observational evidence. Yet as I began my research, I found myself coming up against serious obstacles in practically every area of intellectual activity I investigated.

Most important of these was my growing realization that Darwinism itself seemed very poorly adapted to account for the development of culture, or the overall shape of intellectual history. When I researched the rise of atheism during its "Golden Age" (1789–1989), I was struck by the purposefulness of the contemporary retrieval of the older atheisms of writers such as Xenophanes or Lucretius. These ideas were deliberately reappropriated. Their revival did not just happen; it was *made to happen* in order to achieve a specific goal. The process was strongly teleological, driven by precisely the purpose and intentionality that Darwinian orthodoxy excludes from the evolutionary process.

The same point can be seen in the emergence of the Renaissance, widely regarded as one of the most remarkable developments in the history of Western culture. Its origins lie in Italy during the thirteenth century, although its full blossoming would take place in the following two centuries.[19] The movement expanded from Italy into northern Europe, causing significant changes wherever it took hold. The cultural impact of the movement was immense – for example, the Gothic style of architecture gave way to the classical style, impacting significantly on Western European urban landscapes.[20]

So why did this happen? What explanation may be given for this radical and highly creative redirection of European culture at this time? Since the origins and development of the movement are so well understood, it represents an ideal – indeed, even a critical – case for the application of memetic theory.

Since the pioneering work of P. O. Kristeller, the fundamental basis of the Renaissance is widely accepted to be the critical reappropriation of the culture of ancient Rome (and, to a lesser extent, Athens).[21] Perhaps stimulated by the presence of the remains of classic civilization in Italy, Renaissance theorists advocated the recovery of the rich cultural heritage of the past – the elegant Latin of Cicero; the eloquence of classical rhetoric; the splendor of classical architecture; the philosophies of Plato and Aristotle; the republican political ideals which inspired the Roman constitution.[22] Renaissance writers set about deliberately and systematically adopting these principles, and applying them to their own situation.

It is a fascinating and complex picture, which continues to delight a new generation of scholars. But it does raise some serious difficulties for Dawkins' theory. The origins, development, and transmission of Renaissance humanism – while subject to the inevitable happenstance of history – were *deliberate*, *intentional*, and *planned*. If Darwinism is about copying the instructions (genotype), Lamarckism is about copying the product (phenotype). It would thus seem that Lamarck, rather than Darwin, offers the better account of cultural evolution.

The patterns of development I found in the history of the Renaissance – and, I must add, in most of the other intellectual and cultural phenomena I have studied – is that of the blending of memes, and a clear pattern of intellectual causality which forces us to use a Lamarckian, rather than a neo-Darwinian, understanding of the evolutionary process – assuming, of course, that evolutionary biology has any relevance to the development of culture, or to the history of ideas. The use of such terms as "Darwinian" and "Lamarckian" to describe cultural development may just be downright misleading, implying a fundamental analogy where none – other than the passage of time and the observation of change – really exists.

Dawkins seems to be aware of problems like this. Consider these cautionary comments of 1982:

Memes may partially blend with each other in a way that genes do not. New "mutations" may be "directed" rather than random with respect to evolutionary trends. The equivalent of Weismannism is less rigid for memes than for genes; there may be Lamarckian causal arrows leading from phenotype to replicator, as well as the other way round. These differences may prove sufficient to render the analogy with genetic selection worthless, or positively misleading.[23]

I think this is a fair judgment. If the observational evidence compelled us to conclude that cultural evolution or the development of ideas took place in a Darwinian manner, then that would be the end of the debate. Yet the model is singularly uncompelling, perhaps because it is singularly inappropriate. Biological and cultural evolution may have their points of similarity; they seem, however, to proceed by quite different mechanisms.

## Do Memes Actually Exist?

The second difficulty with the meme idea is that it is inadequately grounded in the evidence. In his preface to Susan Blackmore's *Meme Machine* (1999), Dawkins points out the problems that the "meme" faces if it is to be taken seriously within the scientific community:

Another objection is that we don't know what memes are made of, or where they reside. Memes have not yet found their Watson and Crick; they even lack their Mendel. Whereas genes are to be found in precise locations on chromosomes, memes presumably exist in brains, and we have even less chance of seeing one than of seeing a gene (though the neurobiologist Juan Delius has pictured his conjecture of what a meme might look like).[24]

Dawkins talking about memes is like believers talking about God – an invisible, unverifiable postulate, which helps explain some things about experience, but ultimately lies beyond empirical investigation.

And just what are we to make of the point that "the neurobiologist Juan Delius has pictured his conjecture of what a meme might look like"? I've seen countless pictures of God in many visits to art galleries. And that verifies the concept? Or makes it scientifically plausible? Delius' proposal that a meme will have a single locatable and observable structure as "a constellation of activated neuronal synapses" is purely conjectural, and has yet to be subjected to rigorous empirical investigation.[25] It's one thing to speculate about what something might look like; the real question is whether it is there at all.

In 1993 Dawkins laid down the essence of what constituted a "scientific" approach: "testability, evidential support, precision, quantifiability, consistency, intersubjectivity, repeatability, universality, progressiveness, independence of cultural milieu, and so on."[26] So where is the evidential support for memes? The quantitative analysis? The formulation of criteria by which the meme may be confirmed or eliminated as a useful construct? We await clarification here.

The glaring contrast with the gene will be obvious. Genes can be "seen" and their transmission patterns studied under rigorous empirical conditions. What started off as hypothetical constructs inferred from systematic experiment and observation ended up being observed themselves. The gene was initially seen as a theoretical necessity, in that no other mechanism could explain the relevant observations, before being accepted as a real entity on account of the sheer weight of evidence. But what about memes? The simple fact is that they are, in the first place, *hypothetical constructs*, inferred from observation rather than observed in themselves; in the second place, *unobservable*; and in the third place, more or less *useless* at the explanatory level. This makes their rigorous investigation intensely problematic, and their fruitful application somewhat improbable.

A gene is an observable entity that is well defined at the biological, chemical, and physical levels. Biologically, the gene is a distinct portion of a chromosome; chemically, it consists of DNA; physically, it consists of a double-helix, with a sequence of nucleotides which represent a "genetic code" that can be read and interpreted. Even if genes were never observed, they would continue to be considered a superb theoretical explanation of what can be observed.

The situation with memes is quite different. What are memes? Where are they located? How are they to be described biologically, chemically, and physically? If they were not to be proposed, our understanding of cultural development and the history of ideas would not be disadvantaged. The meme is simply an optional extra, an unnecessary addition to the range of theoretical mechanisms proposed to explain the development of culture. It can be abandoned without difficulty by cultural theorists.

And what about the mechanism by which memes are allegedly transmitted? One of the most important implications of the discovery of the structure of DNA was that it opened the way to an understanding of the mechanism of replication. So what physical mechanism is proposed in the case of the meme? How does a meme cause a memetic effect? Or, to put the question in a more pointed way: how could we even begin to set up experiments to identify and establish the structure of memes, let alone to explore their relation to alleged memetic effects?

Now if memetics was a legitimate evidence-based science, comparable to genetics, there would be no particular difficulty. It might be argued that the memetic observer of cultural evolution is in a situation similar to Darwin in the 1850s – observing patterns which seemed to demand some kind of inherited transmission of traits, even though he had no explanation for such a mechanism. Yet I see no reason for suggesting that memetics offers even a plausible description, let alone an explanation, of the evolution of human culture. While Darwin accumulated a mass of observational evidence in favor of his theories, memetics has yet to make any significant advances on this front. Unsurprisingly, its plausibility is on the wane.

And since the meme is not warranted scientifically, are we to conclude that there is a meme for belief in memes themselves?[27] The meme concept then dies the slow death of self-referentiality, in that, if taken seriously, the idea explains itself as much as anything else. And as the qualifications mount up, the concept loses its plausibility. It's like adding more and more epicycles to the Ptolemaic model of the solar system. What was once a bright, neat idea becomes immensely cumbersome, its initial brilliance fading with every additional qualification added in its defense.

## The Flawed Analogy Between Gene and Meme

Dawkins' argument for both the *existence* and *function* of the meme is based on a proposed analogy between biological and cultural evolution. His implicit assumption seems to be that, since the transmission of culture and the transmission of genes are analogical processes, the well-developed concepts and methods of neo-Darwinism can account for them both. The argument can be set out as follows:

130

> Biological evolution requires a replicator, now known to actually exist, namely the *gene*. So, by analogy:
>
> Cultural evolution also requires a replicator, which is hypothesized to be the *meme*.

It is a brave and bold move. But is it right? Does this analogy actually work? And what is the hard, observational evidence for memes, that demands that we accept this hypothetical concept as a necessary and fruitful means of explaining cultural development?

As has often been demonstrated, analogical argumentation is an essential element of scientific reasoning.[28] The perception of an analogy between A and B is often the starting point for new lines of inquiry, opening up new and exhilarating frontiers. Yet that same perception has often led to scientific dead ends, including the long-abandoned ideas of "calorific" and "phlogiston." As Mario Bunge points out, analogies have a marked propensity to mislead in the sciences.[29] So is this posited analogy between gene and meme in the first place *real*, and in the second *helpful*?

Let's begin by exploring whether the analogy has any basis in fact. The exploration and testing of the limits of scientific analogies is an important and legitimate aspect of the scientific method. In *The Blind Watchmaker* Dawkins provides an eloquent discussion of how science has often advanced by exploring whether a possible analogy may point to something deeper:

Some of the greatest advances in science have come about because some clever person spotted an analogy between a subject that was already understood, and another still mysterious subject. The trick is to strike a balance between too much indiscriminate analogizing on the one hand, and a sterile blindness to fruitful analogies on the other.[30]

Analogies don't always mislead. The problem is working out which ones are fruitful and which are dead ends. In proposing the meme, Dawkins was exploring a potentially significant analogy between biological and cultural evolution, proposing an analogical process or mechanism to account for this. He was not the first to do so, but he communicated it with particular skill.

Exactly the same process of exploring analogies can be seen in Darwin's *Origin of Species*. Darwin spotted what seemed to be an analogy between the way animals were bred to improve certain desirable characteristics, and the way nature seemed to bring about changes. He proposed the idea of "natural selection" as a mechanism within the natural order, analogous to the "artificial selection" of the animal breeding industry.[31] This analogy has turned out to be highly fruitful, but as the history of science demonstrates, there are significant limits to analogical argumentation of this kind.

Remember the ether? Sound and light seemed analogous to many physicists in the nineteenth century. They seemed to behave so similarly. Both were known to be forms of waves, whose speed and wavelength could be determined with a high degree of accuracy. And since the propagation of sound required a medium – such as air or water – then the same had to be true of light as well. The term "ether" was used to designate this mysterious medium, through which light and other electromagnetic radiation traveled.

The Michelson–Morley experiment of 1887 set out to explore the properties of the "luminiferous ether" – that is, the medium through which light was believed to travel. As a result of their experiment, Michelson and Morley came to the remarkable conclusion that "the ether is at rest with regard to the earth's surface."[32] This puzzling result had a number of possible implications. One of these was that there was no "luminiferous ether" in the first place. The analogy with sound had just been pressed too far.

By the 1920s the scientific world had finally come round to the conclusion that light was not the same as sound. There were unquestionably similarities, parallels, and convergences – but these had been overinterpreted, and allowed to create the impression that two different entities were analogous. Even though light and sound did indeed behave in very similar ways in very many contexts, they were completely different things. Light needed no medium; it could travel in a vacuum.

It's a well-known story, and its moral is perfectly clear: analogies can be dangerously misleading. The argument from analogy was seen to have misled here – as it had misled in so many other cases. Quantum theory is an excellent example of a scientific discipline bedeviled by problems arising from the bad use of analogies.[33] And when we move outside the relatively well-defined world of physics into the chaos of human culture, analogies often develop a life of their own, unchecked by the rigid demands of evidence-based argument.

The early case for some physical factor for the transmission of hereditary information – now known as the "gene" – was based on the Mendelian demonstration of the precision of such transmission, and the self-evident fact that there was no other means by which such information could be stored, transmitted, and retrieved. The case of cultural evolution is completely different. All human cultures possess means by which information may be transmitted within existing populations and to subsequent generations – such as books, rituals, institutions, and oral traditions.[34] The notion of a "meme" is functionally redundant, forcing its defenders to make a case by analogy with the gene – yet to downplay the empirically determined biological, chemical, and physical parameters of the gene, which are now an essential aspect of molecular genetics. The plausibility of the meme is thus grounded in a questionable analogical argument, not in overwhelming evidence and observation.

We clearly need the memetic equivalent of the Michelson–Morley experiment – something which will determine, by empirical investigation rather than questionable analogical argumentation, whether memes exist. The present state of research overwhelmingly suggests that memes are the new ether – a redundant hypothesis just waiting to be eliminated.[35] The "meme for memes" may have a high capacity for survival and transmission – but it names nothing in the real world. In fact, in both respects, it seems to be inconveniently similar to Dawkins' God meme.

## The Redundancy of the Meme

Perhaps the most significant criticism of the "meme" concept is that the study of cultural and intellectual development proceeds perfectly well without it. Economic and physical models

– especially information transfer – have proved their worth in this context. The contrast between meme and gene is, once more, painfully obvious: the gene *had* to be postulated, as there was simply no other way of explaining the observational evidence concerning the patterns of transmission of inherited traits. The meme is explanatorily redundant.

Economic models, which treat ideas as "information cascades" or consumer durables, are rather more persuasive and helpful than the unverified meme concept.[36] These models incorporate the "competition" and "extinction" motifs of Darwinian theory, without necessarily endorsing its theories on the origins of innovations. For example, an economic "theory of fads" is considerably more convincing as an explanation of patterns of thought adoption and dispersal than Dawkins' meme.[37] Cultural evolution and intellectual development can often be better understood in terms of a physical, rather than a biological, analogue – such as the transmission of information on random networks.[38] Yet Dawkins does not consider these significant theoretical alternatives in evaluating his meme hypothesis.

The meme is not yet completely dead. Dawkins' canonical memetic statements have been upheld in two major recent publications – Daniel Dennett's *Darwin's Dangerous Idea* (1995) and Susan Blackmore's *The Meme Machine* (1999). Yet the concept of the meme remains so vague and so empirically indeterminate that there is no means by which it can be verified or falsified. In any case, what it proposes to "explain" can be accounted for by other models. Exactly what otherwise puzzling phenomena are accounted for by memes? Dawkins is coy about specifics here, exposing all the more clearly the glaring contrast between this and his brilliant evidence-based defense of his concept of the "selfish gene."

Although now a quarter of a century old, the "science" of memetics has failed to generate a productive research program in mainstream cognitive science, sociology, or intellectual history. On the basis of the evidence available, I can only agree with Martin Gardner's withering criticism of the notion, published in the *Los Angeles Times*:

A meme is so broadly defined by its proponents as to be a useless concept, creating more confusion than light, and I predict that the concept will soon be forgotten as a curious linguistic quirk of little value. To critics, who at the moment far outnumber true believers, memetics is no more than a cumbersome terminology for saying what everybody knows and that can be more usefully said in the dull terminology of information transfer.[39]

Not surprisingly, Dawkins himself has moved on, distancing himself from any suggestion that he offered the meme concept as an explanation of human culture in general.[40] As Daniel Dennett puts it, Dawkins has recently "drawn in his horns slightly."[41] He has retreated from his early optimism, and hinted that the meme hypothesis was simply a useful analogy. Dennett suggests that Dawkins was forced to back off here because he was seen as having become a sociobiologist.[42] I think it rests more on a growing realization of the massive evidential underdetermination of the thesis. The meme concept was either redundant or wrong – and quite possibly both.

## God as a Virus?

Undeterred, Dawkins developed his meme concept in another direction – a virus of the mind. "Memes," Dawkins tells us, can be transmitted "like viruses in an epidemic."[43] Although the connection between a "meme" and a "virus of the mind" is not clarified with the precision we might expect, it is clear that, for Dawkins, the key theme in each case is *replication*. For a virus to be effective, it must possess two qualities: the ability to replicate information accurately, and to obey the instructions which are encoded in the information replicated in this way.[44]

Yet there is also a verbal sleight of hand at work here, a rhetorical device apparently being presented as if it is good science. As everyone knows, viruses are *bad* things; they are contagious, parasitic entities, which exploit their hosts. The rhetorically freighted "argument" that God is a virus amounts

to little more than thinly veiled insinuation, rather than rigorous evidence-based reasoning. Belief in God is proposed as
a malignant infection contaminating otherwise pure minds.
Yet the whole idea founders on the rocks of the absence of
experimental evidence, the subjectivity of Dawkins' personal
value-judgments implicated in assessing what is "good" and
"bad," and the circularity of self-referentiality.

So just what is the experimental evidence that God is
bad for you? Dawkins presumes that it is publicly accepted
within the scientific community that religion debilitates people,
reducing their potential for survival and health. Yet recent
empirical research points to a generally positive interaction
of religion and health. That there are pathological types of
religious belief and behavior is well known; yet this in no way
invalidates the generally positive estimation of religion's impact
on mental health to emerge from evidence-based studies.

Dawkins appears to assume that his readers will rather
uncritically share his own subjective views on the malignancy
of religion, and thus accept his grandiose conclusions without
demur. But they are not grounded in the rigorously evidence-
based analysis, based on objective observation of the impact
of religion on individuals, which is typical of the scientific
enterprise that both Dawkins and I admire. When, one wonders, will popular science catch up with cutting edge research
here?

The implications of this emerging consensus for the "God
as virus" hypothesis are unambiguous. An already tenuous
analogy becomes completely unsustainable. If religion is
reported as having a positive impact on human well-being by
79 percent of recent studies in the field,[45] how can it conceiv-
ably be regarded as analogous to a virus? Viruses are meant
to be bad for you. So just how many viruses have such a
positive impact on their hosts? Far from being something which
reduces the survival value of its host, belief in God is an
additional resource that enhances psychic survival.[46] I have no
doubt that, within the faith-based worldview which shapes
Dawkins' account of reality – atheism – God ought to have
such a negative, detrimental impact on human well-being. But
God does not. The evidence just doesn't fit the theory.

Furthermore, what is the actual experimental evidence for such hypothetical "viruses of the mind"? In the real world, viruses are not known solely by their symptoms; they can be detected, subjected to rigorous empirical investigation, and their genetic structure characterized minutely. In contrast, the "virus of the mind" is hypothetical; posited by a questionable analogical argument, not direct observation; and is totally unwarranted conceptually on the basis of the behavior that Dawkins proposes for it. Can we observe these viruses? What is their structure? Their "genetic code"? Their location within the human body? And, most importantly of all, given Dawkins' interest in their spread, what is their mode of transmission?

There is no experimental evidence that ideas are viruses. Ideas may seem to "behave" in certain respects *as if* they are viruses. But there is a massive gap between analogy and identity – and, as the history of science illustrates only too painfully, most false trails in science are about analogies which were mistakenly assumed to be identities. The "God as virus" slogan, to the extent that it has any scientific validity, might be shorthand for something like "the patterns of diffusion of religious ideas seem to be analogous to those of the spread of certain diseases."

Unfortunately, Dawkins does not give any evidence-based arguments for this, and prefers to conjecture as to the impact of such a hypothetical virus on the human mind. The science just isn't there. In any case, each and every argument that Dawkins adduces for his idea of "God as virus of the mind" can be countered by proposing its counterpart for "atheism as a virus of the mind." Both ideas are equally unsubstantiated and meaningless.

The "thought contagion" metaphor has been developed most thoroughly by Aaron Lynch,[47] who makes the crucially important point that the way in which ideas spread has no necessary relation to their validity or "goodness." As Lynch puts it:

The term "thought contagion" is neutral with respect to truth or falsity, as well as good or bad. False beliefs can spread as thought contagions, but so too can true beliefs. Similarly, harmful ideas can spread as thought contagions, but so too can beneficial ideas . . .

Thought contagion analysis concerns itself primarily with the mechanism by which ideas spread through a population. Whether an idea is true, false, helpful, or harmful are considered mainly for the effects they have on transmission rates.[48]

Neither Dawkins' concepts of the "meme" or the "virus of the mind" – whatever their relationship – really helps us validate or negate ideas, or understand or explain patterns of cultural development. As most working in the area of cultural development have concluded, it is perfectly possible to postulate and study cultural evolution while remaining agnostic to its mechanism. "All we need to do is recognize that cultural inheritance exists, and that its routes are different from the genetic ones."[49]

And what does this have to do with the idea of God? Well, not very much, really. This general approach to the diffusion of ideas may allow some insights about how beliefs spread within a culture. But it can't tell us anything about whether this belief itself is right or wrong, good or bad. This won't stop people drawing such conclusions – but they are not *valid* conclusions. And they are most certainly not *scientific* conclusions.

# Science and Religion: Dialogue or Intellectual Appeasement?

It is widely agreed that in recent years there has been a growing interest in exploring the relation of science and religion. Many are openly speaking about "a new convergence" in the disciplines, opening the way to new insights and understandings.[1] Dawkins has an admirably robust response to this: "To an honest judge," he writes – perhaps with himself modestly in mind? – "the alleged convergence between religion and science is a shallow, empty, hollow, spin-doctored sham."[2]

It's an interesting point of view, but it belongs to another century. In recent years, the scholarly understanding of the historical relationship of science and religion has undergone an intellectual revolution no less than that occasioned by Darwin's *Origin of Species*. Intensive historical scholarly research has demonstrated that the popular notion of a protracted war between church and science which continues to this day is a piece of Victorian propaganda, completely at odds with the facts.[3] Sure, there were individual conflicts, often reflecting institutional politics and personal agendas – such as the Galileo affair – or simply misunderstandings on either or both sides of the debate. But these conflicts are neither typical nor defining.

Dawkins takes a strongly positivist view of science, and links this with the idea that science and religion are necessarily at war with each other. To talk of a rapprochement or convergence between these is therefore for him nothing less than crude "intellectual appeasement."[4] It is thus important to note that this belief is firmly located in the social world of nineteenth-century England, and that both have become severely, even fatally, eroded and discredited with the passing of time. It is understandable that they should still linger in some works of popular science – after all, academic historical scholarship takes a long time to filter down. Yet a serious review of the popular myth of the "warfare of science and religion," so vigorously defended by Dawkins, is long overdue. His popular science has a lot of catching up to do.

To begin our exploration of these issues, we may consider the myth of the permanent "warfare" of science and religion in more detail.

## The "Warfare" of Science and Religion

The history of science makes it clear here that the natural sciences have often found themselves pitted against authoritarianism of any kind. As Freeman Dyson points out in his important essay "The Scientist as Rebel," science often finds itself in "rebellion against the restrictions imposed by the local prevailing culture."[5] Science is thus a subversive activity, almost by definition. For the Arab mathematician and astronomer Omar Khayyam, science was a rebellion against the intellectual constraints of Islam; for nineteenth-century Japanese scientists, science was a rebellion against the lingering feudalism of their culture. In that the West has been dominated by Christianity, it is thus unsurprising that a general tension between science and Western culture could be seen specifically as a confrontation between science and Christianity.

Yet most historians regard religion as having had a generally benign and constructive relationship with the natural sciences in the West. Tensions and conflicts, such as the Galileo controversy, often turned out on closer examination to have more to do with papal politics, ecclesiastical power struggles, and personality issues than with any fundamental tensions between faith and science.[6] Leading historians of science regularly point out that the interaction of science and religion is determined primarily by the specifics of their historical circumstances, and only secondarily by their respective subject matters. There is no universal paradigm for the relation of science and religion, either theoretically or historically. The case of Christian attitudes to evolutionary theory in the late nineteenth century makes this point particularly evident. As the Irish geographer and intellectual historian David Livingstone makes clear in a groundbreaking study of the reception of Darwinism in two very different contexts – Belfast and Princeton – local issues and personalities were often of decisive importance in determining the outcome.[7]

In the eighteenth century, a remarkable synergy developed between religion and the sciences in England. Newton's "celestial mechanics" was widely regarded as at worst consistent with, and at best a glorious confirmation of, the Christian view of God as creator of a harmonious universe. Many members of the Royal Society of London – founded to advance scientific understanding and research – were strongly religious in their outlooks, and saw this as enhancing their commitment to scientific advancement.

Yet all this changed in the second half of the nineteenth century. The general tone of the later nineteenth-century encounter between religion (especially Christianity) and the natural sciences was set by two works: John William Draper's *History of the Conflict between Religion and Science* (1874) and Andrew Dickson White's *The Warfare of Science with Theology in Christendom* (1896). The crystallization of the "warfare" metaphor in the popular mind was unquestionably catalyzed by such vigorously polemical writings.

As a generation of historians has now pointed out, the notion of an endemic conflict between science and religion, so aggressively advocated by White and Draper, is itself socially determined, created in the lengthening shadows of hostility towards individual clergy and church institutions. The interaction of science and religion has been influenced more by their social

141

circumstances than by their specific ideas.[8] The Victorian period itself gave rise to the social pressures and tensions which engendered the myth of permanent warfare between science and religion.

A significant social shift can be discerned behind the emergence of this "conflict" model. From a sociological perspective, scientific knowledge was advocated by particular social groups to advance their own specific goals and interests. There was growing competition between two specific groups within English society in the nineteenth century: the clergy and the scientific professionals. The clergy were widely regarded as an elite at the beginning of the century, with the "scientific parson" a well-established social stereotype. With the appearance of the professional scientist, however, a struggle for supremacy began, to determine who would gain the cultural ascendancy within British culture in the second half of the nineteenth century. The "conflict" model has its origins in the specific conditions of the Victorian era, in which an emerging professional intellectual group sought to displace a group which had hitherto occupied the place of honor.

The "conflict" model of science and religion thus came to prominence at a time when professional scientists wished to distance themselves from their amateur colleagues, and when changing patterns in academic culture necessitated demonstrating its independence from the church and other bastions of the establishment. Academic freedom demanded a break with the church; it was a small step towards depicting the church as the opponent of learning and scientific advance in the late nineteenth century, and the natural sciences as its strongest advocates.

Today, this stereotype of the "warfare of science and religion" lingers on in the backwaters of Western culture. Yet the idea that the natural sciences and religion have been permanently at war with each other is now no longer taken seriously by any historian of science. It is generally accepted that the "warfare" model was developed by religiously alienated individuals in the nineteenth century to help the professional group of natural scientists to break free from ecclesiastical control – a major issue in the intellectual life of Victorian England.[9]

Detailed historical analysis of the origins of the "warfare" model have demonstrated that it is historically located. It does not reflect the fundamental natures or themes of either the natural sciences or Christian theology; it is specifically linked with the social situation of science and religion in Victorian England. With the passing of that particular set of circumstances, that conflict receded.

It is certainly true that some have taken the view that the relation between science and Christian theology is permanently defined, at least in its fundamental respects, by the essential nature of the two disciplines – and, on Dawkins' unsatisfactory reading of the history and philosophy of science, that they are therefore locked into mortal combat, from which science must emerge as the ultimate victor. Underlying these "essentialist" accounts of the interaction of science and religion is the unchallenged assumption that each of these terms designates something fixed, permanent, and essential, so that their mutual relationship is determined by something fundamental to each of the disciplines, unaffected by the specifics of time, place, or culture. But it is simply not so. The relation of science and religion is historically conditioned, bound to the social and intellectual conditions of the age.[10] What we are seeing at present is a growing interest, on both sides of the divide, in seeing how the two disciplines can illuminate and even assist each other's efforts.

The twentieth century has witnessed a vast revision of the simplistic views of the nineteenth century on the nature and limits of the scientific method, and the relation of faith and science. The huge scholarly process of subjecting these traditional views to minute examination has forged a new awareness of possibilities for positive and constructive dialogue and engagement, at a time in the history of Western culture which is showing a new interest in spirituality at every level.

I do wish Dawkins would join in this dialogue, instead of firing off inaccurate, wildly rhetorical salvoes, and lampooning those who disagree with him. Why? One of the defining characteristics of Western culture is the perception of a growing – possibly accelerating – alienation between the humanities and natural sciences, and an increasing cultural unease about where

143

science is taking us. Back in 1959, C. P. Snow observed that the gulf between the arts and sciences had become so pronounced that it was necessary to speak of two distinct and non-interactive cultures in Western society:

The intellectual life of the whole of Western society is increasingly being split into two polar groups ... Literary intellectuals at one pole ... at the other scientists, and as the most representative, the physical scientists. Between the two a gulf of mutual incomprehension.[11]

If anything, things seem to have got worse since then. The once relatively civilized disagreements between the natural sciences and the humanities seem to have given way to something approaching a shooting war. Recent works dealing with the cultural impact of science show a growing polarization between the disciplines. The possibility of reconciliation – or even a constructive dialogue – seems to diminish year by year. And Dawkins is one of those who some accuse of making things worse.[12] It doesn't need to be like this.

Cautious and careful exploration of issues has been replaced by the megaphone diplomacy of the ideologues. On the one hand, we have those who insist that science is totally objective and neutral in its methods and goals, and dismiss those who express anxieties about those methods or goals as "anti-scientific" or "defilers of science."[13] On the other, we have those who argue that the sciences have failed to appreciate the extent to which they are constituted by social and cultural forces, and who excoriate what they see as pretentious claims to privilege – such as the claim that the sciences offer the best account of things.[14]

*Unweaving the Rainbow* marks a significant change in Dawkins' writing style. Instead of offering a popular exposition of Darwinian evolutionary theory, linked with speculation on its metaphysical and religious implications, we find a sustained engagement with a cultural agenda. Part of the book's content – not to mention its title – derive from Dawkins' 1997 C. P. Snow Lecture at Cambridge, in which he explored the hostility of the English Romantic poet John Keats (1795–1821) towards Isaac Newton's mechanical philosophy.[15] This deep suspicion towards scientific analysis is best seen in Keats' 1820 poem "Lamia," in which he protests against reducing the beautiful and awesome phenomena of nature to the basics of scientific theory, thus allegedly emptying nature of its beauty and mystery, and reducing it to something cold and clinical:

> Do not all charms fly
> At the mere touch of cold philosophy?
> There was an awful rainbow once in heaven:
> We know her woof, her texture; she is given
> In the dull catalogue of common things.
> Philosophy will clip an Angel's wings.

*Unweaving the Rainbow* is a triumphalist manifesto for the cultural independence of the sciences. It is a robust defense of the values of the Enlightenment, untroubled by the less appealing aspects of the scientific enterprise – such as the links between scientific research and military applications – in the face of what Dawkins sees as outbursts of irrationality in Western culture. Nor does Dawkins bother to note the darker side of the Enlightenment, which has so troubled many thinkers of the late twentieth century – such as its demand for the enforcement of uniformity, and its intolerance for deviation from what is declared to be "rational."

*Unweaving the Rainbow* is also a work of no small importance for the present book, which focuses on Dawkins' religious views. Two issues stand out as being of major significance:

1 Dawkins argues that the sciences lead to a model of the universe which is "not a superstitious, small-minded, parochial model filled with spirits and hobgoblins, astrology and magic, glittering with fake crocks of gold at where the rainbow ends."[16] In contrast, the religious view of nature is presented as being so ugly that it could not lead anyone to aesthetically pleasing conclusions. Religion is said to be aesthetically deficient, leading to the impoverishment of nature, and a diminution of the natural human sense of wonder and mystery evoked by the universe, and its scientific investigation.

2   His elimination of any transcendent dimension to nature as aesthetically redundant and intellectually untenable. Science is said to get rid of such meaningless notions as "purpose," "God," and so forth. Nothing is lost by their elimination, except the deviousness that keeps the psychics, astrologers, and other peddlers of dishonest nonsense in business.

It is the first of these criticisms of religion that is the more important, and we may turn immediately to explore it in greater detail.

## The Poky Little Medieval Universe of Religion

One of Dawkins' persistent complaints about religion is that it is aesthetically deficient. Its view of the universe is limited, impoverished, and unworthy of the wonderful reality known by the sciences:

The universe is genuinely mysterious, grand, beautiful, awe-inspiring. The kinds of views of the universe which religious people have traditionally embraced have been puny, pathetic, and measly in comparison to the way the universe actually is. The universe presented by organized religions is a poky little medieval universe, and extremely limited.[17]

The logic of this bold assertion is rather hard to follow, and its factual basis astonishingly slight. The "medieval" view of the universe may indeed have been more limited and restricted than modern conceptions. Yet this has nothing to do with religion, either as cause or effect. It reflected the science of the day, largely based upon Aristotle's treatise *de caelo* ("on heaven"). If the universe of religious people in the Middle Ages was indeed "poky," it was because they trusted the best cosmologists of the day to tell them what it was like. This, they were assured, was scientific truth, and they accepted it. They took it on trust. They were naive enough to assume that what their science textbooks told them was right. Precisely that trust in science and scientists which Dawkins commends so uncritically led them to weave their theology around some- one else's view of the universe. They didn't know about such things as "radical theory change in science," which causes twenty-first century people to be cautious about investing too heavily in the latest scientific theories, and much more critical of those who base worldviews upon them.

Medieval conceptions of the universe were largely based on a Ptolemaic model of the planetary system, which located the earth at the center of a vast, ordered cosmic mechanism.[18] This is vividly depicted in Hartmann Schedel's *Nuremberg Chronicle* (1493), one of the most popular and technologically advanced printed books of the late Middle Ages. On this grand view of the universe, the earth stood at the center of a series of concentric spheres, each of which rotates round the earth according to its own predetermined rhythms. Beyond them lies the "empyrean" – a vast, eternal, infinite, and formless void. Christian theologians assumed that this was where para- dise was located, often on the basis of questionable traditional arguments.[19] Popular depictions of this vision of the universe, such as the *Nuremberg Chronicle*, depict God and the saints as dwelling in this region. It's not today's model of the solar system, and is wrong at just about every point. It's certainly "medieval," but it's hardly a "poky little universe." Most medieval writers that I have read on the topic found the thought of cosmic vastness to be really rather awesome – even on a Ptolemaic model of the heavens.

The implication of Dawkins' unsubstantiated criticism is that a religious view of reality is deficient and impoverished in comparison with his own. There is no doubt that this con- sideration is an important factor in generating and maintaining his atheism. Yet his analysis of this issue is disappointingly thin and unpersuasive. One of the common themes of much reli- gious writing in the English language from about 1550 to 1850 is that the scientific investigation of the grandeur and glory of nature leads to an enhanced appreciation of the glory of God.[20] Although I see no reason to impute such a base motive to such writers, it was in their interest to exaggerate the beauty and wonders of the created order, so that a correspondingly greater

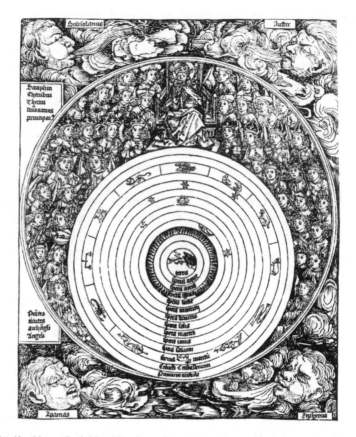

Plate 10    A late medieval vision of the universe. Hartmann Schedel's *Nuremberg Chronicle* (1493) depicts the earth as lying in a fixed position at the center of the universe, surrounded by a series of spheres defining the orbits of the Moon, Mercury, Venus, the Sun, Mars, Jupiter, and Saturn. The "empyrean" lies beyond the fixed stars. Photo AKG-Images

vision of God might be had. The very slight historical evidence that Dawkins brings forward in support of his extravagant excoriation of religious visions of reality, whether in *Unweaving the Rainbow* or elsewhere, amounts to little more than an observation that our understanding of the vastness and complexity of the universe has increased in recent years.

A Christian approach to nature identifies three ways in which a sense of awe comes about in response to what we observe.

1 An immediate sense of wonder at the beauty of nature. This is evoked *immediately*. This "leap of the heart" that William Wordsworth described on seeing a rainbow in the sky occurs *before* any conscious theoretical reflection on what it might imply. To use psychological categories, this is about *perception*, rather than *cognition*. I can see no good reason for suggesting that believing in God in any way diminishes this sense of wonder. Dawkins' argument at this point is so underdetermined by evidence and so utterly implausible that I fear I must have misunderstood it.

2 A derived sense of wonder at the mathematical or theoretical representation of reality which arises from this. Dawkins also knows and approves of this second source of "awed wonder," but seems to imply that religious people "revel in mystery and feel cheated when it is explained."[21] They don't; a new sense of wonder emerges, which I will explain in a moment.

3 A further derived sense of wonder at what the natural world points to. One of the central themes of Christian theology is that the creation bears witness to its creator: "The heavens declare the glory of the Lord!" (Psalm 19:1). For Christians, to experience the beauty of creation is a sign or pointer to the glory of God, and is to be particularly cherished for this reason. Dawkins excludes any such transcendent reference from within the natural world.

Dawkins suggests that a religious approach to the world misses out on something.[22] Having read *Unweaving the Rainbow*, I still haven't worked out what this is. A Christian reading of the world denies nothing of what the natural sciences tell us, except the naturalist dogma that reality is limited to what may be known through the natural sciences. If anything, a Christian engagement with the natural world adds a richness which I find quite absent from Dawkins' account of things, offering a new motivation for the study of nature. After all, John Calvin (1509–64) commented on how much he envied those who studied physiology and astronomy, which allowed a direct engagement with the wonders of God's creation. The invisible and intangible God, he pointed out, could be appreciated through studying the wonders of nature. Perhaps the greatest difference between science and religion thus lies not in how they begin, nor even in how they proceed, but in how they end.

In a moment, we will give thought to a Christian reading of nature. But first, we need to pause, and explore this sense of "awe" which so many people experience in an encounter with the wonders of nature.

## The Concept of Awe

In recent years, a new interest has arisen in the concept of "awe." The idea has featured prominently in theology, sociology, and philosophy. For example, Rudolf Otto spoke of the "numinous" – a *mysterium tremendum et fascinans* which inspired awe on the part of those who experienced it.[23] Such an experience can be both profoundly positive and terrifyingly negative, and frequently reduces the subject to a state of silence or confusion. More recently, the concept has begun to attract the attention of psychologists,[24] who have noted that a range of stimuli triggers an experience of awe, including "religious encounters, charismatic political leaders, natural objects, and even patterns of light."

In a recent groundbreaking study, Dacher Keltner and Jonathan Haidt developed a prototype approach to the experience of awe, which has at its heart two distinctive features: *vastness* and *accommodation*.[25] Vastness, they argue, refers to "anything that is experienced as being much larger than the self, or the self's ordinary level of experience or frame of reference." It may refer simply to physical size, or to more subtle markers of vastness, such as social signs or symbolic markers. Accommodation refers to the process identified by Jean Piaget (1896–1980), professor of genetic and experimental psychology at the University of Geneva from 1940–71. Piaget defined this as the process by which human mental structures undergo an adjustment in the face of the challenge posed by new experiences. Thus it would be possible to

SCIENCE AND RELIGION

experience a sense of awc through rcalization of the "breadth and scope of a grand theory" – such as evolutionary theory itself.

We propose that prototypical awe involves a challenge to or negation of mental structures when they fail to make sense of an experience of something vast. Such experiences can be disorientating and even frightening ... They also often involve feelings of enlightenment and even rebirth, when mental structures expand to accommodate truths never before known. We stress that awe involves a *need* for accommodation, which may or not be satisfied. The success of one's attempt at accommodation may partially explain why awe can be both terrifying (when one fails to understand) and enlightening (when one succeeds).[26]

On the basis of this approach, the human sense of awe at the vastness of the universe, or the dramatic beauty of a natural landscape or feature (such as a rainbow), could be enhanced by grasping the theoretical foundations or implications of what was being observed. This resonates with Dawkins' belief – which is also mine – that the theoretical representations of reality are in themselves beautiful, and capable of evoking awe on account of their complexity or their capacity to invoke a "big picture" view of things. This is unquestionably the case with theories which propose a larger vision of things – a list of theories which includes, but is not limited to, Darwinism, Marxism, and Christian theology.

## The Mind of God

Christian theology does not in any way detract from a natural appreciation of the beauty and wonder of the world; if anything, it adds to it. As I pointed out, there are three levels at which Christianity affirms a sense of wonder about nature: (1) through an immediate encounter with its vast beauty; (2) through the theoretical explanation and representation of nature; and (3) through nature's capacity to point to God as its creator. I assume that the first of these is uncontroversial, and will discuss the remaining two in what follows.

The unsubstantiated allegation that Christian theology holds that the "explanation" of natural phenomena robs them of divine significance is total nonsense. The fact that we are able to develop such theories in the first place, along with the mathematical beauty of the resulting theories, is firmly grounded in a Christian worldview. The theoretical physicist John Polkinghorne explores the implications of this point as follows:

We are so familiar with the fact that we can understand the world that most of the time we take it for granted. It is what makes science possible. Yet it could have been otherwise. The universe might have been a disorderly chaos rather than an orderly cosmos. Or it might have had a rationality which was inaccessible to us ... There is a congruence between our minds and the universe, between the rationality experienced within and the rationality observed without.[27]

That human beings have been remarkably successful in investigating and grasping something of the structure and workings of the world is beyond dispute. Precisely why the rationality of the world should be so accessible to human beings remains rather more puzzling. Polkinghorne is quite clear as to how Christianity might offer an explanation of this observation:

If the deep-seated congruence of the rationality present in our minds with the rationality present in the world is to find a true explanation, it must surely lie in some more profound reason which is the ground of both. Such a reason would be provided by the Rationality of the Creator.[28]

In developing this point, Polkinghorne draws on resources from deep within the Christian tradition, which stresses that God endowed humanity with intelligence and reason both to investigate the world, and to discover God. Precisely the same point was made by the astronomer Johann Kepler, at the dawn of the Scientific Revolution. Since geometry had its origins in the mind of God, it was only to be expected that the created order would conform to its patterns:

In that geometry is part of the divine mind from the origins of time, even from before the origins of time (for what is there in God that is not also from God?) has provided God with the patterns for the creation of the world, and has been transferred to humanity with the image of God.[29]

On this reading of things, which is typical of the Christian tradition, the theoretical representation of reality can itself be seen as peering into the mind of God. Dawkins, I have no doubts, will wish to dispute this interpretation of theory. Yet his suggestion that Christianity *necessarily* or *characteristically* places a total embargo on the theoretical representation of the world is simply untenable, unsubstantiated by the evidence.

More importantly, Christianity argues that nature is to be seen as an "image of divine things" – something which somehow points to God himself, enabling us to see nature in a new light. While not denying anything of what Dawkins affirms about the beauty of the world, this perspective simply adds to it, by seeing nature as a pointer towards the greater beauty of God. The wonder of the creator can be known through the created order. This point was made by the thirteenth-century theologian Bonaventure, a great admirer of Francis of Assisi and his love for every aspect of nature:

The creatures of the world lead the souls of the wise and contemplative to the eternal God, since they are the shadows, echoes and pictures; the vestiges, images and visible images of the most powerful, wise and best first principle of that eternal origin, light and fulness; of that productive, exemplary and order-inducing art. They are set before us in order that we might know God. We are given signs by God . . . every creature is by its very nature and kind of depiction and likeness of that eternal wisdom.[30]

This idea that nature elicits the praise and knowledge of God underlies Romanticism, which sought to reestablish a connection between nature and the transcendent. Romanticism viewed the development of the mechanistic model of the universe, which it associated with Newton, with great distress.[31] Something had been lost – a sense of *mystery*. As Dawkins raises this question in *Unweaving the Rainbow*, we may explore this in more detail.

## Mystery, Insanity, and Nonsense

Dawkins is a splendid representative of the no-nonsense, "one rationality fits all" approach of the Enlightenment. Perhaps this is most obvious in his discussion of "mystery" – a category which he cheerfully, if a little prematurely, reduces to "plain insanity or surrealist nonsense."[32] We can make sense of things – or, if we can't make sense of things right now, the relentless advance of science will make this possible sooner or later. Given enough time, anything can happen. Religious people who talk about "mystery" are just irrational mystics who are too lazy or frightened to use their minds properly.

It's a recognizable caricature of the idea of "mystery." But it's still a caricature. Here's what a theologian means when using the word "mystery": something which is true and possesses its own rationality – yet which the human mind finds it impossible to grasp fully. Some years ago, I started learning Japanese. I didn't get very far. The language uses two syllabaries, has a vocabulary which bears little relation to any of the languages that I knew, and a syntax that seemed completely illogical to my Western way of thinking. In short: I couldn't make sense of it. But my failure to grasp the Japanese language represents a failure on my part. Those who know the language assure me that it is rational and intelligible; it's just that I can't get my mind around it.

There is no way that the concept of "mystery" means "an irrationality," except in the sense that it may be counter-intuitive. It may lie beyond the present capacity of human reason to grasp; that does not mean it is contrary to reason, as Thomas Aquinas emphasized. The human mind is just too limited to grasp the totality of such a reality, and we must therefore do what we can, while recognizing our limits. We're not God, and hence find what John Donne called "the immense weight of divine glory" difficult to cope with. And it's not just an issue in the area of theology. Any attempt to engage with the immensity of nature – such as the seemingly vast time scale of Darwinian evolution – faces the same problems, and makes the use of both the word and the idea of "mystery" entirely appropriate in the natural sciences. Dawkins himself knows this, as is clear from his derisive comment on postmodern critics of the sciences:

Modern physics teaches us that there is more to truth than meets the eye; or than meets the all too limited human mind, evolved as it was to cope with medium-sized objects moving at medium speeds through medium distances in Africa. In the face of these profound and sublime mysteries, the low-grade intellectual poodling of pseudo-philosophical poseurs seems unworthy of adult attention.[33]

My point precisely.

Quantum mechanics is an excellent example of an area of science where the category of "mystery" seems entirely appropriate. It is something that we believe to be true, and to possess a deep rationality of its own – but which it often seems impossible to get our minds around. I certainly found my mathematics pressed to its limits when specializing in this discipline at Oxford in the academic year 1972–3. Dawkins concurs, noting in particular how its conclusions "can be disturbingly counter-intuitive."[34]

The point here is that both the scientific and religious communities can be thought of as attempting to wrestle with the ambiguities of experience, and offering what are accepted as the "best possible explanations" for what is observed, accepting the intellectual difficulties that are demanded on account of the evidence which demands that we think in this way. The analysis of experience can lead to the generation of conceptualities which are often very complex, and occasionally quite counter-intuitive. Many more unreflective natural scientists hostile to religion deride the complexity of its conceptualities. Science, they argue, deals with simple ideas, and avoids such extravagant ventures into such realms. Others, however, who have given more careful thought to the matter, are not so sure.

The Princeton philosopher of science Bas van Fraassen is intensely skeptical of those who suggest that science is justifiably simple whereas religion is unjustifiably complex; once more, quantum theory is cited as an example:

Do the concepts of the Trinity, the soul, haecceity, universals, prime matter, and potentiality baffle you? They pale beside the unimaginable otherness of closed space-times, event-horizons, EPR correlations, and bootstrap models.[35]

Fraassen clearly considers that the conceptual and imaginative demands of some areas of modern physics exceed those traditionally associated with even the most labyrinthine theological and philosophical systems of the Middle Ages. His point is that an empirical engagement with the world of experience and phenomena throws up theoretical concepts which are far from simple, yet which appear to be inevitable if the phenomena are to be preserved.

For an orthodox Christian theologian, the doctrine of the Trinity is the inevitable outcome of intellectual engagement with the Christian experience of God; for the physicist, equally abstract and bewildering concepts emerge from wrestling with the world of quantum phenomena. But both are committed to sustained intellectual engagement with those phenomena, in order to derive and develop theories or doctrines which can be said to do justice to them, preserving rather than reducing them.

Dawkins' most reflective account of "mystery" is found in *Unweaving the Rainbow*, which explores the place of wonder in an understanding of the sciences. While maintaining Dawkins' core hostility to religion, the work acknowledges the importance of a sense of awe and wonder in driving people to want to understand reality. Dawkins singles out the poet William Blake as an obscurant mystic, who illustrates why religious approaches to mystery are pointless and sterile. Dawkins locates Blake's many failings in an understandable – but misdirected – longing to delight in a mystery:

The impulses to awe, reverence and wonder which led Blake to mysticism . . . are precisely those that lead others of us to science. Our interpretation is different but what excites us is the same. The mystic is content to bask in the wonder and revel in a mystery that we were not "meant" to understand. The scientist feels the same wonder, but is restless, not content; recognizes the mystery as profound, then adds, "But we're working on it."[36]

So there isn't actually a problem with the word or the category of "mystery." The question is whether we choose to wrestle with it, or take the lazy and complacent view that this is conveniently off-limits.

Now let's agree that William Blake was a somewhat colorful character, with decidedly odd ideas. He can hardly be taken as representative of mainline Christianity. Blake was regarded by many of his family and friends as showing symptoms of an incipient insanity, not least because of his "visions." Who can read his poem "Milton" – which includes, incidentally, the famous song "Jerusalem" – without being fazed by Blake's graphic description of how the spirit of the poet John Milton fell vertically from heaven, before entering him through the tarsus of his left foot? But Blake is not typical of Christian theology – a discipline he opposed on several grounds, by the way, not least its tendency towards rationalism.

Traditionally, Christian theology has been well aware of its limits, and has sought to avoid excessively confident affirmations in the face of mystery. Yet, at the same time, Christian theology has never seen itself as totally reduced to silence in the face of divine mysteries. Nor has it prohibited intellectual wrestling with "mysteries" as destructive or detrimental to faith. As the nineteenth-century Anglican theologian Charles Gore rightly insisted:

Human language never can express adequately divine realities. A constant tendency to apologize for human speech, a great element of agnosticism, an awful sense of unfathomed depths beyond the little that is made known, is always present to the mind of theologians who know what they are about, in conceiving or expressing God. "We see," says St. Paul, "in a mirror, in terms of a riddle;" "we know in part." "We are compelled," complains St. Hilary, "to attempt what is unattainable, to climb where we cannot reach, to speak what we cannot utter; instead of the mere adoration of faith, we are compelled to entrust the deep things of religion to the perils of human expression."[37]

A perfectly good definition of Christian theology is "taking rational trouble over a mystery" – recognizing that there may be limits to what can be achieved, but believing that this intellectual grappling is both worthwhile and necessary. It just means being confronted with something so great that we cannot fully comprehend it, and so must do the best that we can with the analytical and descriptive tools at our disposal.

Come to think of it, that's what the natural sciences aim to do as well. Perhaps it's no wonder that there is such a growing interest in the dialogue between science and religion.

## Conclusion

This book has barely scratched the surface of a series of fascinating questions raised by the writings of Richard Dawkins. Some of these are directly, others indirectly, religious in nature. I am conscious that I have failed to deal with any of them in the detail that they rightly demand. I have opened up some questions for further discussion, and have not settled anything – except that the issues raised in this book are important and interesting, and that further discussion is needed. Dawkins raises all the right questions, and gives some interesting answers. They're not particularly reliable answers, admittedly, unless you happen to believe that religious people are science-hating fools who are into "blind faith" and other unmentionable things in a big way.

This book aims to move the discussion on, and draw a line under the often unreliable account of the relation of science and religion that Dawkins offers. An evidence-based approach to this question is much more complex and much more *interesting* than Dawkins' "path of simplicity and straight thinking." There are, as Dawkins rightly points out, areas of tension, which must be acknowledged and confronted; yet alongside them there is an immense potential for intellectual synergy and the discovery of fresh perspectives on reality.

I'm sure that we all have much to learn by debating with each other, graciously and accurately. The question of whether there is a God, and what that God might be like, has not

– despite the predictions of overconfident Darwinians – gone away since Darwin, and remains of major intellectual and personal importance. Some minds on both sides of the argument may be closed; the evidence and the debate, however, are not. Scientists and theologians have so much to learn from each other. Listening to each other, we might hear the galaxies sing.[38] Or even the heavens declaring the glory of the Lord (Psalm 19:1).

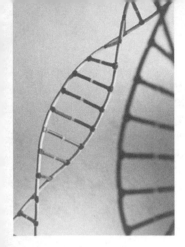

# Acknowledgments

This work has been gestating for many years, and owes much to many. I owe a particular debt to senior academic colleagues who have read this work in draft form, and were generous in their comments: Denis Alexander, R. J. Berry, Francis Collins, Simon Conway Morris, David C. Livingstone, Alvin Plantinga, Michael Ruse, and especially Joanna McGrath. I myself am responsible for any remaining errors of fact or interpretation. Oxford University kindly provided clarification on some important points of detail. The John Templeton Foundation has supported research in science and religion for several years, and I – along with many others working in this field – am indebted to them for their assistance and encouragement. Although this work was originally suggested back in 1978 by an editor at Oxford University Press, I finally decided to entrust it to Blackwell Publishers, with whom I have worked happily for many years. Blackwell has been all that a good publisher should be, and I especially thank Rebecca Harkin for her encouragement and guidance throughout this project.

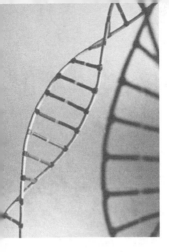

# Notes

## Encountering Dawkins: A Personal Account

1 Tom Wolfe, "The Great Relearning." In *Hooking Up*, 140–5. London: Jonathan Cape, 2000.

2 *A Devil's Chaplain*, 16.

3 For some examples, see Alister E. McGrath, Christopher G. Morgan, and George K. Radda, "Photobleaching: A Novel Fluorescence Method for Diffusion Studies in Lipid Systems." *Biochimica et Biophysica Acta* 426 (1976): 173–85; idem, "Positron Lifetimes in Phospholipid Dispersions." *Biochimica et Biophysica Acta* 466 (1976): 367–72.

4 It took me the best part of twenty-five years to figure out how to do it: for the outcome, see Alister McGrath, *A Scientific Theology*, 3 vols. Grand Rapids, MI: Eerdmans, 2001–3. For a more basic introduction, see Alister McGrath, *The Science of God: An Introduction to Scientific Theology*. Grand Rapids, MI: Eerdmans, 2004.

5 The one I initially had greatest hopes for was Pierre Rousselot, "Petit théorie du développement du dogme." *Recherches de science religieuse* 53 (1965): 355–90.

6 I was not the only one to be so excited in this way by Dawkins' new idea: see Stephen Shennan, *Genes, Memes and Human*

*History: Darwinian Archaeology and Cultural Evolution*. London: Thames & Hudson, 2002, 7.

7 I later wondered if I had made too much of this incident in Darwin's intellectual development: see Frank J. Sulloway, "Darwin and His Finches: The Evolution of a Legend." *Journal of the History of Biology* 15 (1982): 1–53.

8 Michael Ruse, "Through a Glass, Darkly." *American Scientist* 91 (2003): 554–6.

9 Cited by Robert Fulford, "Richard Dawkins Talks Up Atheism with Messianic Zeal." *National Post* November 25, 2003.

10 These argue that Jesus of Nazareth was either mad, bad, or God. As he wasn't the first or the second, he must be the third. The argument works by proposing only three solutions to a hugely complex issue, and dismissing two of them. The chief criticism made of the argument is its simplistic refusal to consider alternatives beyond those on which it depends.

11 Kim Sterelny, *Dawkins vs. Gould: Survival of the Fittest*. Cambridge: Icon Books, 2001. His ideas are, of course, dealt with in various articles and sections of books: for example, see Michael Poole, "A Critique of Aspects of the Philosophy and Theology of Richard Dawkins." *Science and Christian Belief* 6 (1994): 41–59; Luke Davidson, "Fragilities of Scientism: Richard Dawkins and the Paranoid Idealization of Science." *Science as Culture* 9 (2000): 167–99; Holmes Rolston, *Genes, Genesis and God: Values and Their Origins in Natural and Human History*. Cambridge: Cambridge University Press, 1999; Keith Ward, *God, Chance and Necessity*. Oxford: One World, 1996, 105–30.

12 See Fulford, "Richard Dawkins Talks Up Atheism with Messianic Zeal."

13 For related questions concerning Darwin's view of God, see Cornelius G. Hunter, *Darwin's God : Evolution and the Problem of Evil*. Grand Rapids, MI: Brazos Press, 2001.

14 "Alternative Thought for the Day"; BBC Radio 4, August 14, 2003.

15 Richard Dawkins, "A Survival Machine." In *The Third Culture*, edited by John Brockman, 75–95. New York: Simon & Schuster, 1996.

16 *A Devil's Chaplain*, 34.

## Chapter 1　The Selfish Gene: A Darwinian View of the World

1　*A Devil's Chaplain*, 196.
2　For a critical yet appreciative account of Tinbergen, see Hans Kruuk, *Niko's Nature: The Life of Niko Tinbergen, and His Science of Animal Behaviour*. Oxford: Oxford University Press, 2003. For Dawkins' personal evaluation of Tinbergen's significance, see Marian S. Dawkins, Tim Halliday, and Richard Dawkins, *The Tinbergen Legacy*. London: Chapman & Hall, 1991.
3　Richard Dawkins, "The Ontogeny of a Pecking Preference in Domestic Chicks." *Zeitschrift für Tierpsychologie* 25 (1968): 170–86.
4　The key paper was published in two parts in 1964: William Hamilton, "The Genetic Evolution of Social Behaviour." *Journal of Theoretical Biology* 7 (1964): 1–16; 17–52.
5　*River out of Eden*, 19.
6　*Oxford University Calendar 2003–4*. Oxford: Oxford University Press, 2003, 77.
7　For further details, see James A. Secord, *Victorian Sensation: The Extraordinary Publication, Reception, and Secret Authorship of Vestiges of the Natural History of Creation*. Chicago: University of Chicago Press, 2000.
8　On which see James A. Secord, "Nature's Fancy: Charles Darwin and the Breeding of Pigeons." *Isis* 72 (1981): 163–86.
9　The theory is set out in his *The Variation of Animals and Plants under Domestication*, 2 vols. London: John Murray, 1868.
10　See Conway Zirkle, *The Early History of the Idea of the Inheritance of Acquired Characters and of Pangenesis*. Philadelphia, PA: American Philosophical Society, 1946.
11　Gregor Johann Mendel, "Versuche über Pflanzen-Hybriden." *Verhandlungen des naturforschenden Vereins in Brünn* 4 (1866): 3–47.
12　See, for example, Carl Correns, "G. Mendels Regel über das Verhalten der Nachkommenschaft Der Rassenbastarde." *Berichte der deutschen botanischen Gesellschaft* 18 (1900): 158–68.
13　See, for example, the reports of G. von Niessl, published in *Verhandlungen des naturforschenden Vereins in Brünn* 41 (1902): 18–21; 44 (1905): 5–9.
14　B. E. Bishop, "Mendel's Opposition to Evolution and to Darwin." *Journal of Heredity* 87 (1996): 205–13. It needs to be said, however, that this represents nothing more than an inference on Bishop's part, in that Mendel only refers to Darwin four times in

his writings, and these references indicate neither support nor hostility towards Darwin's views.

15  Ronald A. Fisher, *The Genetical Theory of Natural Selection*. Oxford: Clarendon Press, 1930.

16  F. di Trocchio, "Mendel's Experiments: A Reinterpretation." *Journal of the History of Biology* 24 (1991): 485–519.

17  The best review in English is Daniel J. Fairbanks and Bryce Rytting, "Mendelian Controversies: A Botanical and Historical Review." *American Journal of Botany* 88 (2001): 737–52.

18  More specifically, a copy of the second German edition of 1863, based on the third English edition of 1861. Only two passages are double-marked in this way.

19  Charles Darwin, *On the Origin of Species by Natural Selection*, 3rd edn. London: John Murray, 1861, 296.

20  Vítezslav Orel, *Gregor Mendel: The First Geneticist*. Oxford: Oxford University Press, 1996, 193.

21  *A Devil's Chaplain*, 67–9.

22  *The Selfish Gene*, 34.

23  Oswald Avery, Colin MacLeod, and Maclyn McCarty, "Studies on the Chemical Nature of the Substance Inducing Transformation of Pneumococcal Types: Induction of Transformation by a Desoxyribonucleic Acid Fraction Isolated from Pneumococcus Type III." *Journal of Experimental Medicine* 79 (1944): 137–58.

24  Francis H. C. Crick and James D. Watson, "Molecular Structure of Nucleic Acids: A Structure for Deoxyribose Nucleic Acid." *Nature* 171 (1953): 737–8.

25  For further details, see such works as Anthony J. F. Griffiths, *An Introduction to Genetic Analysis*, 7th edn. New York: W. H. Freeman, 2000; idem, *Modern Genetic Analysis: Integrating Genes and Genomes*, 2nd edn. New York: W. H. Freeman, 2002.

26  Richard D. Alexander, *Darwinism and Human Affairs*. London: Pitman, 1980, 38.

27  *The Selfish Gene*, 34.

28  *The Selfish Gene*, 35.

29  *The Selfish Gene*, 34.

30  Zhiyan Zhou and Shaolin Zheng, "The Missing Link in Ginkgo Evolution." *Nature* 423 (2003): 821–2.

31  Jacques Monod, *Chance and Necessity: An Essay on the Natural Philosophy of Modern Biology*. New York: Alfred A. Knopf, 1971, 114.

32  Monod, *Chance and Necessity*, 118.

33  *The Blind Watchmaker*, 49.

34  *A Devil's Chaplain*, 81. This does not, by the way, imply that all evolutionary change is adaptive.

35  *The Selfish Gene*, 21.

36  Richard Dawkins, "Replicators and Vehicles." In *Current Problems in Sociobiology*, edited by King's College Sociobiology Group, 45–64. Cambridge: Cambridge University Press, 1982. Other evolutionary biologists use different terminology: for example, David Hull prefers to speak of "interactors" and "replicators." See David L. Hull, *Science as a Process: An Evolutionary Account of the Social and Conceptual Development of Science*. Chicago: University of Chicago Press, 1990.

37  *The Extended Phenotype*, 239.

38  Seymour Benzer, "The Elementary Units of Heredity." In *The Chemical Basis of Heredity*, edited by W. D. McElroy and B. Glass, 70–93. Baltimore, MD: Johns Hopkins University Press, 1957.

39  *The Selfish Gene*, 28.

40  George C. Williams, "A Package of Information." In *The Third Culture*, edited by John Brockman, 38–50. New York: Simon & Schuster, 1995.

41  George C. Williams, *Adaptation and Natural Selection: A Critique of Some Current Evolutionary Thought*. Princeton, NJ: Princeton University Press, 1966, 25.

42  It must be noted at this point that Dawkins' proposal is much more adept at accounting for the modification of the characteristics of existing species than for the generation of new species. See Steven Rose, "The Rise of Neurogenetic Determinism." In *Consciousness and Human Identity*, edited by John Cornwell, 86–100. Oxford: Oxford University Press, 1998.

43  Richard Dawkins, "Replicator Selection and the Extended Phenotype." *Zeitschrift für Tierpsychologie* 47 (1978): 61–76.

44  *The Extended Phenotype*, 199–200.

45  *The Blind Watchmaker*, 259.

46  For example, see L. N. Benachenhou, P. Forterre, and B. Labedan, "Evolution of Glutamate Dehydrogenase Genes: Evidence for Two Paralogous Protein Families and Unusual Branching Patterns of the Archaebacteria in the Universal Tree of Life." *Journal of Molecular Evolution* 36 (1993): 335–46; Elizabeth Pennisi, "Is It Time to Uproot the Tree of Life?" *Science as Culture* 284 (1999): 1305–7.

47  See, for example, K. Henze, C. Schnarrenberger, and W. Martin, "Endosymbiotic Gene Transfer: A Special Case of Horizontal Gene Transfer Germane to Endosymbiosis, the Origins of

Organelles and the Origins of Eukaryotes." In *Horizontal Gene Transfer*, edited by M. Syvanen and C. Kado, 343–52. London: Academic Press, 2001.

48 Mary Midgley, "Gene-Juggling." *Philosophy* 54 (1979): 439–58.
49 A point made regularly by Dawkins' critics within the evolutionary biology community: see, for example, Steven Rose, "The Rise of Neurogenetic Determinism." In *Consciousness and Human Identity*, edited by John Cornwell, 86–100. Oxford: Oxford University Press, 1998.
50 For Dawkins' response, see Richard Dawkins, "In Defence of Selfish Genes." *Philosophy* 56 (1981): 556–73.
51 Richard Dawkins, "Selective Pecking in the Domestic Chick." D.Phil. Thesis, Oxford University, 1966, 183–5.
52 *The Selfish Gene*, 196.
53 For an exploration of this point, see the essay "Darwin Triumphant: Darwinism as Universal Truth," in *A Devil's Chaplain*, 78–90.
54 For the difference between the two, see Karl-Otto Apel, "The Erklären–Verstehen Controversy in the Philosophy of the Natural and Human Sciences." In *Contemporary Philosophy: A New Survey*, edited by G. Floistad, 19–49. The Hague: Nijhof, 1982.
55 For an illuminating example, see Luke Davidson, "Fragilities of Scientism: Richard Dawkins and the Paranoid Idealization of Science." *Science as Culture* 9 (2000): 167–99. For a more general postmodern response to scientific criticism of cultural accounts of science, see Brian Martin, "Social Construction of an 'Attack on Science'." *Social Studies of Science* 26 (1996): 161–73.
56 *River out of Eden*, 96–9.
57 Richard Dawkins, "Alternative Thought for the Day," BBC Radio 4, August 14, 2003.
58 Charles Darwin, *The Descent of Man*, 2nd edn. London: John Murray, 1882, 619.
59 For comment, see Maurice Mandelbaum, *History, Man, and Reason: A Study in Nineteenth-Century Thought*. Baltimore, MD: Johns Hopkins University Press, 1971, 77–88; Dov Ospovat, *The Development of Darwin's Theory: Natural History, Natural Theology, and Natural Selection, 1838–1859*. Cambridge: Cambridge University Press, 1995, 229–35.
60 *A Devil's Chaplain*, 20–5.
61 See here Paul L. Farber, *The Temptations of Evolutionary Ethics*. Berkeley, CA: University of California Press, 1994, 136. Farber comments that Huxley's "ethics was a projection of his

values onto the history of man," so that his "naturalism assumed the vision he pretended to discover".

62 Richard Weikart, "A Recently Discovered Darwin Letter on Social Darwinism." *Isis* 86 (1995): 609–11.
63 *A Devil's Chaplain*, 10–11.
64 *The Selfish Gene*, 200–1. The first edition (1976) ended at this point; the second edition (1989) added two additional chapters.
65 For Dawkins' comments, see *Unweaving the Rainbow*, 286–90; *A Devil's Chaplain*, 74–7.
66 For some reflections, not dissimilar to Dawkins, see Geoffrey Miller, *The Mating Mind: How Sexual Choice Shaped the Evolution of Human Nature*. London: Vintage, 2001.
67 *The Selfish Gene*, 109–22.

## Chapter 2   The Blind Watchmaker: Evolution and the Elimination of God?

1 *River out of Eden*, 133.
2 An excellent study of this issue may be found in Michael Ruse, *Darwin and Design: Does Evolution Have a Purpose?* Cambridge, MA: Harvard University Press, 2003.
3 *The Blind Watchmaker*, 43.
4 *Climbing Mount Improbable*, 64.
5 *Climbing Mount Improbable*, 126–79.
6 The index, of course, is not exhaustive: see, for example, the brief (and somewhat puzzling) discussion of God found in *The Blind Watchmaker*, 141. But the omission is interesting.
7 Richard Dawkins, "A Survival Machine." In *The Third Culture*, edited by John Brockman, 75–95. New York: Simon & Schuster, 1996.
8 Francis S. Collins, "Faith and the Human Genome." *Perspectives on Science and Christian Faith* 55 (2003): 142–53.
9 See his 1883 letter to Charles A. Watts, publisher of the *Agnostic Annual*. For further comment, see Alan Willard Brown, *The Metaphysical Society: Victorian Minds in Crisis, 1869–1880*. Oxford: Oxford University Press, 1947.
10 Stephen Jay Gould, "Impeaching a Self-Appointed Judge." *Scientific American* 267, 1 (1992): 118–21.
11 *A Devil's Chaplain*, 149.
12 For the issues, which apply equally well to natural and social sciences, see the classic study of Gilbert Harman, "The Inference

to the Best Explanation." *Philosophical Review* 74 (1965): 88–
95. A more recent and extended discussion worth noting is Ernan
McMullin, *The Inference That Makes Science*. Milwaukee, WI:
Marquette University Press, 1992.

13 See James T. Cushing, *Quantum Mechanics: Historical Conting-ency and the Copenhagen Hegemony*. Chicago: University of Chicago Press, 1994.
14 *The Blind Watchmaker*, 46–51.
15 *The Blind Watchmaker*, 47.
16 Friedrich Waismann, *The Principles of Linguistic Philosophy*. London: Macmillan, 1965, 60.
17 *The Blind Watchmaker*, 50.
18 *Climbing Mount Improbable*, 75.
19 For what follows, see Etienne Gilson, *The Christian Philosophy of St. Thomas Aquinas*. Notre Dame, IN: University of Notre Dame Press, 1994.
20 For background, see Margaret J. Osler, *Divine Will and the Mechanical Philosophy: Gassendi and Descartes on Contingency and Necessity in the Created World*. Cambridge: Cambridge University Press, 1994.
21 *The Blind Watchmaker*, 4–6.
22 See James R. Jacob and Margaret C. Jacob. "The Anglican Origins of Modern Science: The Metaphysical Foundations of the Whig Constitution." *Isis* 71 (1980): 251–67.
23 See, for example, Umberto Eco, *The Aesthetics of Thomas Aquinas*. London: Radius, 1988; Patrick Sherry, *Spirit and Beauty: An Introduction to Theological Aesthetics*. Oxford: Clarendon Press, 1992.
24 For some reflections, see John Hedley Brooke, *Science and Religion: Some Historical Perspectives*. Cambridge: Cambridge University Press, 1991.
25 See the careful study of H. H. Odom, "The Estrangement of Celestial Mechanics and Religion." *Journal of the History of Ideas* 27 (1966): 533–58.
26 James E. Force, "The Breakdown of the Newtonian Synthesis of Science and Religion: Hume, Newton and the Royal Society." In *Essays on the Context, Nature and Influence of Isaac Newton's Theology*, edited by R. H. Popkin and J. E. Force, 143–63. Dordrecht: Kluwer Academic Publishers, 1990.
27 John Gascoigne, "From Bentley to the Victorians: The Rise and Fall of British Newtonian Natural Theology." *Science in Context* 2 (1988): 219–56.

28  William Paley, *Works*. London: Wm. Orr, 1849, 25.

29  *The Blind Watchmaker*, 5.

30  For an example, see Dov Ospovat, *The Development of Darwin's Theory: Natural History, Natural Theology, and Natural Selection, 1838–1859*. Cambridge: Cambridge University Press, 1995.

31  On which see Aileen Fyfe, "The Reception of William Paley's *Natural Theology* in the University of Cambridge." *British Journal for the History of Science* 30 (1997): 321–35.

32  See Edward Manier, *The Young Darwin and His Cultural Circle: A Study of Influences Which Helped Shape the Language and Logic of the First Drafts of the Theory of Natural Selection*. Dordrecht: Reidel, 1978.

33  John Henry Newman, *The Idea of a University*. London: Longmans, Green, 1907, 450–1. For the background, see Fergal McGrath, *The Consecration of Learning: Lectures on Newman's Idea of a University*. Dublin: Gill, 1962.

34  Newman, *Idea of a University*, 454.

35  James R. Moore, *The Post-Darwinian Controversies: A Study of the Protestant Struggle to Come to Terms with Darwin in Great Britain and America, 1870–1900*. Cambridge: Cambridge University Press, 1979.

36  R. S. S. Baden-Powell, *Essays on the Spirit of the Inductive Philosophy*. London: Longman, Brown, Green, and Longmans, 1855. For an excellent analysis of this thinker, see Pietro Corsi, *Science and Religion: Baden Powell and the Anglican Debate*. Cambridge: Cambridge University Press, 1988.

37  See here Aidan Nichols, *From Newman to Congar: The Idea of Doctrinal Development from the Victorians to the Second Vatican Council*. Edinburgh: T. & T. Clark, 1990.

38  On this, see Tarsicius van Bavel, "The Creator and the Integrity of Creation in the Fathers of the Church." *Augustinian Studies* 21 (1990): 1–33.

39  See Frances M. Young, "Adam and Anthropos: A Study of the Interaction of Science and the Bible in Two Anthropological Treatises of the Fourth Century." *Vigiliae Christianae* 37 (1983): 110–40.

40  A much more satisfactory account may be found in John Hedley Brooke, "The Relations between Darwin's Science and His Religion." In *Darwinism and Divinity*, edited by John Durant, 40–75. Oxford: Blackwell, 1985.

41  Edward Aveling, *The Religious Views of Charles Darwin*. London: Freethought, 1883.

42　One of the great urban myths concerning Darwin is linked with Aveling: confusion over the true addressee of Darwin's letter of rejection to Aveling led to the widespread belief that Karl Marx himself had requested permission to dedicate *Das Kapital* to Darwin. Aveling was assembling Marx's correspondence at the time, and the Darwin letter seems to have been mis-filed. See Ralph Colp, Lewis Feuer, and P. Thomas Carroll, "On the Darwin–Marx Correspondence." *Annals of Science* 33 (1976): 383–94.

43　For the best analysis, see Frank Burch Brown, *The Evolution of Darwin's Religious Views*. Macon, GA: Mercer University Press, 1986.

44　For a study of the causes of Darwin's illness, characterized by intermittent "excitement, violent shivering and vomiting attacks," see Ralph E. Colp, *To be an Invalid: The Illness of Charles Darwin*. Chicago: University of Chicago Press, 1977.

45　This has been beautifully documented by Randal Keynes, *Annie's Box: Charles Darwin, His Daughter and Human Evolution*. London: Fourth Estate, 2001.

46　Donald Fleming, "Charles Darwin, the Anaesthetic Man." *Victorian Studies* 4 (1961): 219–36.

47　Letter to Asa Gray (1860): *The Life and Letters of Charles Darwin*, 3 vols. London: John Murray, 1887, vol. 2, 310–12.

48　See U. C. Knoepflmacher, *Religious Humanism and the Victorian Novel: George Eliot, Walter Pater, and Samuel Butler*. Princeton, NJ: Princeton University Press, 1970.

49　For an excellent overview of this moral revulsion, see Geoffrey Rowell, *Hell and the Victorians: A Study of the Nineteenth-Century Theological Controversies Concerning Eternal Punishment and the Future Life*. Oxford: Clarendon Press, 1974.

50　See here works such as Howard R. Murphy, "The Ethical Revolt against Christian Orthodoxy in Early Victorian England." *American Historical Review* 60 (1955): 800–17.

51　See Bernard V. Lightman, *The Origins of Agnosticism: Victorian Unbelief and the Limits of Knowledge*. Baltimore, MD: Johns Hopkins University Press, 1987.

52　Text in Thomas H. Huxley, "An Episcopal Trilogy." In *Science and Christian Tradition: Essays*, 126–59. London: Macmillan, 1894.

53　See, for example, David N. Livingstone, *Darwin's Forgotten Defenders: The Encounter between Evangelical Theology and Evolutionary Thought*. Grand Rapids, MI: Eerdmans, 1987.

54 See the two important recent studies: David N. Livingstone, "B. B. Warfield, the Theory of Evolution and Early Fundamentalism." *Evangelical Quarterly* 58 (1986): 69–83; David N. Livingstone and Mark A. Noll. "B. B. Warfield (1851–1921): A Biblical Inerrantist as Evolutionist." *Isis* 91 (2000): 283–304.

55 For details, see George Marsden, *Fundamentalism and American Culture: The Shaping of Twentieth Century Evangelicalism 1870–1925.* New York: Oxford University Press, 1980.

56 James Orr, "Science and Christian Faith." In *The Fundamentals*, vol. 1, 334–47. 4 vols. Los Angeles: Bible Institute of Los Angeles, 1917.

57 See the excellent biography by his daughter, Joan Fisher Box, *R. A. Fisher: The Life of a Scientist.* New York: Wiley, 1978.

58 R. A. Fisher, "The Renaissance of Darwinism." *The Listener* 37 (1947): 1009.

59 Gould, "Impeaching a Self-Appointed Judge."

## Chapter 3 Proof and Faith: The Place of Evidence in Science and Religion

1 Richard E. Nisbett and Lee D. Ross, *Human Inference: Strategies and Shortcomings of Social Judgment.* Englewood Cliffs, NJ: Prentice-Hall, 1980, 192.

2 Nisbett and Ross, *Human Inference*, 169.

3 Keith Ward, *God, Chance and Necessity.* Oxford: One World, 1996, 99–100.

4 *The Selfish Gene*, 198.

5 *The Selfish Gene*, 330 (this passage was added to the second edition).

6 The lecture had no agreed title, and was published under the title "Lions 10, Christians Nil" in Volume 1, Number 8 (December 1994) of an electronic journal entitled "The Nullafidian," which describes itself as "The E-Zine of Atheistic Secular Humanism and Freethought," formerly known as "Lucifer's Echo." There is no pagination. The journal appears to have ceased publication in March 1996.

7 *A Devil's Chaplain*, 117.

8 *A Devil's Chaplain*, 248.

9 W. H. Griffith-Thomas, *The Principles of Theology.* London: Longmans, Green, 1930, xviii. Faith thus includes "the certainty of evidence" and the "certainty of adherence"; it is "not blind, but intelligent" (xviii–xix).

171

10   See, for example, Dimitry V. Pospielovsky, *A History of Marxist-Leninist Atheism and Soviet Anti-Religious Policies*. New York: St. Martin's Press, 1987.

11   Debate between Richard Dawkins and Steve Pinker at Westminster Central Hall, London, on 19 February 1999, chaired by Tim Radford, science correspondent of the *Guardian*.

12   *The Selfish Gene*, 330.

13   Dawkins contrasts a series of "caricatures" of Darwinism with the real thing in *The Blind Watchmaker*, 308–11. It would be instructive to do the same for caricatures of religious belief, in which I fear Dawkins might feature rather prominently, and then compare them with authentic statements from mainline theologians and statements of faith, such as Pope John Paul II's encyclical letter "Faith and Reason" (September 1998).

14   See David Corfield and Jon Williamson, *Foundations of Bayesianism*. Dordrecht: Kluwer Academic, 2001; Eric D. Green and Peter Tillers, *Probability and Inference in the Law of Evidence: The Uses and Limits of Bayesianism*. Dordrecht: Kluwer Academic, 1988.

15   Elliott R Sober, "Modus Darwin." *Biology and Philosophy* 14 (1999): 253–78.

16   Richard Swinburne, *The Resurrection of God Incarnate*. Oxford: Clarendon Press, 2003.

17   *The Selfish Gene*, 198.

18   *The Selfish Gene*, 1.

19   *Climbing Mount Improbable*, 68.

20   See, for example, Wesley C. Salmon, *Scientific Explanation and the Causal Structure of the World*. Princeton, NJ: Princeton University Press, 1984.

21   Paul Kitcher, "Explanatory Unification and the Causal Structure of the World." In *Scientific Explanation*, edited by P. Kitcher and W. Salmon, 410–505. Minneapolis: University of Minnesota Press, 1989.

22   See especially Richard P. Feynman, *What Do You Care What Other People Think?* London: Unwin Hyman, 1989; Richard P. Feynman, *The Meaning of It All*. London: Penguin Books, 1999.

23   Timothy Shanahan, "Methodological and Contextual Factors in the Dawkins/Gould Dispute over Evolutionary Progress." *Studies in History and Philosophy of Science* 31 (2001): 127–51.

24   Ludwig Wittgenstein, *Lectures and Conversations on Aesthetics, Psychology and Religious Belief*. Oxford: Blackwell, 1966. "If I had to say what is the main mistake made by philosophers . . . I

would say that it is that when language is looked at, what is looked at is a form of words and not the use made of the form of words."

25  Madeleine Sigman-Grant and Jaime Morita, "Defining and Interpreting Intakes of Sugars." *American Journal of Clinical Nutrition* 78 (2003): 815S–826S.

26  Richard Dawkins, "In Defence of Selfish Genes." *Philosophy* 56 (1981): 556–73. For Midgley's original article, see Mary Midgley, "Gene-Juggling." *Philosophy* 54 (1979): 439–58. For her response to Dawkins' criticisms, see Mary Midgley, "Selfish Genes and Social Darwinism." *Philosophy* 58 (1983): 365–77.

27  I have in mind such works as Richard Swinburne, *The Coherence of Theism*. Oxford: Clarendon Press, 1977; Nicholas Wolterstorff, *Reason within the Bounds of Religion*. Grand Rapids, MI: Eerdmans, 1984; Alvin Plantinga, *Warranted Christian Belief*. Oxford: Oxford University Press, 2000.

28  *A Devil's Chaplain*, 139.

29  For details, see Robert D. Sider, "Credo Quia Absurdum?" *Classical World* 73 (1978): 417–19.

30  Tertullian, *de paenitentia* v, 4.

31  James Moffat, "Tertullian and Aristotle." *Journal of Theological Studies* 17 (1916): 170–1.

32  See especially Robert D. Sider, *Ancient Rhetoric and the Art of Tertullian*. Oxford: Oxford University Press, 1971, 56–9.

33  Tertullian, *de paenitentia* i, 2. "Quippe res dei ratio quia deus omnium conditor nihil non ratione providit disposuit ordinavit, nihil enim non ratione tractari intellegique voluit."

34  *A Devil's Chaplain*, 117.

35  See the excellent study of Lawrence Badash, "The Completeness of Nineteenth-Century Science." *Isis* 63 (1973): 48–58.

36  W. D. Niven (ed.), *The Scientific Papers of James Clerk Maxwell*, 2 vols. Cambridge: Cambridge University Press, 1980, vol. 2, 244.

37  Max Planck, *A Scientific Autobiography*. New York: Philosophical Library, 1949, 8.

38  Robert A. Millikan, *The Autobiography of Robert A. Millikan*. New York: Houghton, Mifflin, 1950, 23–4. On Millikan, see Robert Hugh Pargon, *The Rise of Robert Millikan: Portrait of a Life in American Science*. Ithaca, NY: Cornell University Press, 1982.

39  Simon Newcomb, "The Place of Astronomy among the Sciences." *The Sidereal Messenger* 7 (1888): 69–70.

40  William Bateson, *Mendel's Principles of Heredity*. Cambridge: Cambridge University Press, 1909, 2–3. For Bateson's own work on sweet peas, see William Bateson, E. R. Saunders, and R. C. Punnett, "Further Experiments on Inheritance in Sweet Peas and Stocks: Preliminary Account." In *Scientific Papers of William Bateson*, edited by R. C. Punnett, 139–41. Cambridge: Cambridge University Press, 1905.

41  Thomas S. Kuhn, *The Structure of Scientific Revolutions*, 2nd edn. Chicago: University of Chicago Press, 1970.

42  For the biological sciences, see the points raised by Sylvia Culp and Philip Kitcher, "Theory Structure and Theory Change in Contemporary Molecular Biology." *British Journal for the Philosophy of Science* 40 (1989): 459–83.

43  Karl R. Popper. *Unended Quest: An Intellectual Autobiography*. London: Fontana, 1976. He changed his mind over the next few years: see Karl R. Popper, letter to *New Scientist* 87: 611, August 21, 1980. For a survey of the issues, see David N. Stamos, "Popper, Falsifiability, and Evolutionary Biology." *Biology and Philosophy* 11 (1996): 161–91.

44  *A Devil's Chaplain*, 81. Dawkins suggests that it may be possible to isolate a "core Darwinism" which is relatively resistant to this kind of historical erosion.

45  The work which sparked this off is generally thought to have been Alan G. Gross, *The Rhetoric of Science*. Cambridge, MA: Harvard University Press, 1990; second edition, 1996. For some reflections on the implications of this point, see Gillian Beer, *Darwin's Plots: Evolutionary Narrative in Darwin, George Eliot, and Nineteenth-Century Fiction*, 2nd edn. Cambridge: Cambridge University Press, 2000.

46  Daniel C. Dennett, *Darwin's Dangerous Idea: Evolution and the Meaning of Life*. New York: Simon & Schuster, 1995, 471.

47  Simon Hattenstone, "Darwin's Child." *Guardian*, February 10, 2003.

48  Richard Dawkins, "Selective Pecking in the Domestic Chick." D.Phil. Thesis, Oxford University, 1966.

49  See W. R. Miller and C. E. Thoreson, "Spirituality, Religion and Health: An Emerging Research Field." *American Psychologist* 58 (2003): 24–35.

50  The "religion as pathology" view originates largely from the pseudo-scientific studies of Sigmund Freud: see Frederick Crews (ed.), *Unauthorized Freud: Doubters Confront a Legend*. New York: Penguin Books, 1998. On the growing recognition of the

positive social and personal impact of faith, see Rodney Stark, *For the Glory of God: How Monotheism Led to Reformations, Science, Witch-Hunts, and the End of Slavery*. Princeton, NJ: Princeton University Press, 2003.

51 For example, see Harold G. Koenig and Harvey J. Cohen, *The Link between Religion and Health: Psychoneuroimmunology and the Faith Factor*. Oxford: Oxford University Press, 2001; A. J. Weaver, L. T. Flannelly, J. Garbarino, C. R. Figley, and K. J. Flannelly, "A Systematic Review of Research on Religion and Spirituality in the *Journal of Traumatic Stress*, 1990–99." *Mental Health, Religion and Culture* 6 (2003): 215–28.

52 Koenig and Cohen, *The Link between Religion and Health*, 101.

53 Cited in Kim A. McDonald, "Oxford U. Professor Preaches Darwinian Evolution to Skeptics." *Chronicle of Higher Education*, November 29, 1996.

54 *A Devil's Chaplain*, 185.

55 *A Devil's Chaplain*, 128–45.

56 Acceptance speech on being awarded the 2000 Templeton Prize for Progress in Religion; reprinted in *The Tablet* (May 20, 2000), 234.

57 Stéphane Courtois, *The Black Book of Communism: Crimes, Terror, Repression*. Cambridge, MA: Harvard University Press, 1999.

58 For the details, see Alister McGrath, *The Twilight of Atheism: The Rise and Fall of Disbelief in the Modern World*. New York: Doubleday, 2004.

59 Louis Frederick Fieser and Mary Fieser, *Advanced Organic Chemistry*. London: Chapman & Hall, 1968.

60 *A Devil's Chaplain*, 243–5.

## Chapter 4 Cultural Darwinism? The Curious "Science" of Memetics

1 Joseph Poulshock, "Universal Darwinism and the Potential of Memetics." *Quarterly Review of Biology* 77 (2002): 174–5.

2 Donald T. Campbell, "Blind Variation and Selective Retention in Creative Thought as in Other Knowledge Processes." *Psychological Review* 67 (1960): 380–400.

3 Donald T. Campbell, "A General 'Selection Theory' as Implemented in Biological Evolution and in Social Belief-Transmission-with-Modification in Science." *Biology and Philosophy* 3 (1988):

413–63. The term was first introduced by Campbell in 1974; this article sets out a later exposition of the notion.

4 Charles J. Lumsden and Edward O. Wilson, *Genes, Mind, and Culture: The Coevolutionary Process*. Cambridge, MA: Harvard University Press, 1981.

5 See, for example, Susan J. Blackmore, *The Meme Machine*. Oxford: Oxford University Press, 1999.

6 *A Devil's Chaplain*, 117.

7 William Lloyd Newell, *The Secular Magi: Marx, Freud, and Nietzsche on Religion*. New York: Pilgrim Press, 1986.

8 *A Devil's Chaplain*, 117.

9 F. T. Cloak, "Is a Cultural Ethology Possible?" *Human Ecology* 3 (1975): 161–81. An earlier version of this article appeared in *Research Previews* 15 (1968): 37–47. For another perspective, see L. L. Cavalli-Sforza, "Cultural Evolution." *American Zoologist* 26 (1986): 845–55.

10 *The Selfish Gene*, 192. Similarly, the word "memetic" was coined, paralleling "genetic"; once more, the intention was to stress that both biological and cultural evolution could be accounted for by "units of replication" or "units of transmission."

11 *The Selfish Gene*, 192.

12 They are all examples of what Cloak terms "m-culture" – in other words, things which arise through the impact of ideas on the environment – where one would expect them to be "i-culture" (again, in Cloak's terms).

13 *The Extended Phenotype*, 109.

14 For an excellent presentation of this point, see Gary Cziko, *Without Miracles: Universal Selection Theory and the Second Darwinian Revolution*. Cambridge, MA: MIT Press, 1995.

15 *The Selfish Gene*, 193.

16 On which see John A. Ball, "Memes as Replicators." *Ethology and Sociology* 5 (1984): 145–61.

17 *A Devil's Chaplain*, 145.

18 Simon Conway Morris, *Life's Solution: Inevitable Humans in a Lonely Universe*. Cambridge: Cambridge University Press, 2003, 324.

19 There is a huge literature. For a useful introduction, see Charles G. Nauert, *Humanism and the Culture of Renaissance Europe*. Cambridge: Cambridge University Press, 1995.

20 See, for example, Norbert Huse, Wolfgang Wolters, and Edmund Jephcott, *The Art of Renaissance Venice: Architecture, Sculpture, and Painting, 1460–1590*. Chicago: University of Chicago

Press, 1990; James S. Ackerman, *Distance Points: Essays in Theory and Renaissance Art and Architecture*. Cambridge, MA: MIT Press, 1991.

21  See, for example, Paul Oskar Kristeller, *Renaissance Thought: The Classic, Scholastic, and Humanistic Strains*. New York: Harper & Row, 1961.

22  For the general issue, see Ronald G. Witt, *In the Footsteps of the Ancients: The Origins of Humanism from Lovato to Bruni*. Leiden: Brill, 2000.

23  *The Extended Phenotype*, 112.

24  *A Devil's Chaplain*, 124.

25  Juan D. Delius, "The Nature of Culture." In *The Tinbergen Legacy*, edited by M. S. Dawkins, T. R. Halliday, and R. Dawkin, 75–99. London: Chapman & Hall, 1991.

26  *A Devil's Chaplain*, 145.

27  Alan Costall, "The 'Meme' Meme." *Cultural Dynamics* 4 (1991): 321–35.

28  Daniel Rothbart, "The Semantics of Metaphor and the Structure of Science." *Philosophy of Science* 51 (1984): 595–615.

29  Mario Bunge, *Method, Model, and Matter*. Dordrecht: D. Reidel, 1973, 125–6.

30  *The Blind Watchmaker*, 195.

31  See Robert M. Young, "Darwin's Metaphor and the Philosophy of Science." *Science as Culture* 16 (1993): 375–403.

32  A. A. Michelson and E. W. Morley. "On the Relative Motion of the Earth and Luminiferous Ether." *American Journal of Science* 34 (1887): 333–45.

33  Mario Bunge, "Analogy in Quantum Theory: From Insight to Nonsense." *British Journal for the Philosophy of Science* 18 (1967): 265–86.

34  There is a huge literature, including works such as Niklas Luhmann, *Love as Passion: The Codification of Intimacy*. Stanford, CA: Stanford University Press, 1998; Vera Schwarcz, *Bridge across Broken Time: Chinese and Jewish Cultural Memory*. New Haven, CT: Yale University Press, 1998; John Lowney, *The American Avant-Garde Tradition: William Carlos Williams, Postmodern Poetry, and the Politics of Cultural Memory*. Lewisburg, PA: Bucknell University Press, 1997.

35  There are some very interesting alternative proposals for the interaction of genes and culture set out in William H. Durham, *Coevolution: Genes, Culture, and Human Diversity*. Stanford, CA: Stanford University Press, 1991.

36 See, for example, S. Bikhchandani, D. Hirshleifer, and I. Welch, "Learning from the Behavior of Others: Conformity, Fads, and Informational Cascades." *Journal of Economic Perspectives* 12 (1998): 151–70.

37 S. Bikhchandani, D. Hirshleifer, and I. Welch, "A Theory of Fads, Fashion, Custom, and Cultural Change as Informational Cascades." *Journal of Political Economy* 100 (1992): 992–1026. Dawkins fails to explore this issue in his account of "crazes," which he analyses very superficially using an epidemiological model: *A Devil's Chaplain*, 136–7.

38 See, for example, D. J. Watts, "A Simple Model of Information Cascades on Random Networks." *Proceedings of the National Academy of Sciences* 99 (2002): 5766–71. The implications of this as an analogue for the transmission of ideas in a cultural system will be obvious.

39 Martin Gardner, "Kilroy Was Here." *Los Angeles Times*, March 5, 2000.

40 *A Devil's Chaplain*, 127.

41 Daniel C. Dennett, *Evolution and the Meaning of Life*. New York: Simon & Schuster, 1995, 361. It is worth noting that the meme hypothesis is still advocated in *Unweaving the Rainbow*, 304–10.

42 Dennett, *Darwin's Dangerous Idea*, 361–2.

43 *A Devil's Chaplain*, 121. For a religious response to this suggestion, see John W. Bowker, *Is God a Virus?: Genes, Culture, and Religion*. London: SPCK, 1995.

44 *A Devil's Chaplain*, 135.

45 Harold G. Koenig and Harvey J. Cohen, *The Link between Religion and Health: Psychoneuroimmunology and the Faith Factor*. Oxford: Oxford University Press, 2002, 101.

46 Kenneth I. Pargament, *The Psychology of Religion and Coping: Theory, Research, Practice*. New York: Guilford Press, 1997.

47 Aaron Lynch, *Thought Contagion: How Belief Spreads Through Society*. New York: Basic Books, 1996.

48 Aaron Lynch, "An Introduction to the Evolutionary Epidemiology of Ideas." *Biological Physicist* 3, no. 2 (2003): 7–14.

49 Stephen Shennan, *Genes, Memes and Human History: Darwinian Archaeology and Cultural Evolution*. London: Thames & Hudson, 2002, 63. Shennan cites the work of Luca Cavalli-Sforza and Marcus Feldman in support: *Cultural Transmission and Evolution: A Quantitative Approach*. Princeton, NJ: Princeton University Press, 1981.

## Chapter 5    Science and Religion: Dialogue or Intellectual Appeasement?

1    See, for example, Michael Ruse, *Can a Darwinian Be a Christian? The Relationship Between Science and Religion.* Cambridge: Cambridge University Press, 2001.

2    *A Devil's Chaplain,* 151.

3    Two publications have been especially important in forcing this radical review of the popular viewpoint: David C. Lindberg and Ronald L. Numbers, *God and Nature: Historical Essays on the Encounter Between Christianity and Science.* Berkeley: University of California Press, 1986; Edward Grant, *The Foundations of Modern Science in the Middle Ages: Their Religious, Institutional, and Intellectual Contexts.* Cambridge: Cambridge University Press, 1996.

4    *A Devil's Chaplain,* 149.

5    Freeman Dyson, "The Scientist as Rebel." In *Nature's Imagination: The Frontiers of Scientific Vision,* edited by John Cornwell, 1–11. Oxford: Oxford University Press, 1995.

6    Mario Biagioli, *Galileo, Courtier: The Practice of Science in the Culture of Absolutism.* Chicago: University of Chicago Press, 1993.

7    David N. Livingstone, "Darwinism and Calvinism: The Belfast–Princeton Connection." *Isis* 83 (1992): 408–28.

8    Colin A. Russell, "The Conflict Metaphor and Its Social Origins." *Science and Christian Faith* 1 (1989): 3–26.

9    Frank M. Turner, "The Victorian Conflict Between Science and Religion: A Professional Dimension." *Isis* 69 (1978): 356–76.

10    For a sustained critique of this position, richly illustrated with historical case studies, see John Brooke and Geoffrey Cantor, *Reconstructing Nature: The Engagement of Science and Religion.* Edinburgh: T. & T. Clarke, 1998.

11    C. P. Snow, *The Two Cultures and the Scientific Revolution.* Cambridge: Cambridge University Press, 1959, 3. Snow's analysis is open to challenge at points, especially the way in which he contrasts Goethe and Newton: see Hannelore Schwedes, "Goethe *contra* Newton." *Westermanns pädagogische Beiträge* 27 (1975), 63–73.

12    See Hugh Aldersley-Williams, "The Misappliance of Science." *New Statesman,* September 13, 1999.

13    See, for example, Paul R. Gross and Norman Levitt, *Higher Superstition: The Academic Left and Its Quarrels with Science.* Baltimore, MD: Johns Hopkins University Press, 1998.

14 See the issues raised by Brian Martin, "Social Construction of an 'Attack on Science'." *Social Studies of Science* 26 (1999): 161–73.

15 *Unweaving the Rainbow*, xv.

16 *Unweaving the Rainbow*, 312.

17 Richard Dawkins, "A Survival Machine." In *The Third Culture*, edited by John Brockman, 75–95. New York: Simon & Schuster, 1996.

18 By far the best study is Edward Grant, *Planets, Stars and Orbs: The Medieval Cosmos, 1200–1687*. Cambridge: Cambridge University Press, 1996.

19 Grant, *Planets, Stars and Orbs*, 169–85, 371–89.

20 An excellent example being the earlier works of John Ruskin; see Michael Wheeler, *Ruskin's God*. Cambridge: Cambridge University Press, 1999.

21 *Unweaving the Rainbow*, xiii. See also his extended discussion, ranging from traditional religions to New Age movements, at 114–79.

22 *Unweaving the Rainbow*, xii.

23 Rudolf Otto, *The Idea of the Holy: An Inquiry into the Non-Rational Factor in the Idea of the Divine and Its Relation to the Rational*, 2nd edn. Oxford: Oxford University Press, 1978.

24 Richard S. Lazarus, *Emotion and Adaptation*. New York: Oxford University Press, 1991; Paul Ekman, "An Argument for Basic Emotions." *Cognition and Emotion* 6 (1992): 169–200.

25 Dacher Keltner and Jonathan Haidt, "Approaching Awe, a Moral, Spiritual and Aesthetic Emotion." *Cognition and Emotion* 17 (2003): 297–314.

26 Dacher Keltner and Jonathan Haidt, "Approaching Awe, a Moral, Spiritual and Aesthetic Emotion." *Cognition and Emotion* 17 (2003): 297–314. The quote can be found at page 304.

27 John Polkinghorne, *Science and Creation: The Search for Understanding*. London: SPCK, 1988, 20–1.

28 Polkinghorne, *Science and Creation*, 22.

29 Johann Kepler, *Gesammelte Werke*, ed. Max Caspar. Munich: C. H. Beck, 1937–83, vol. 6, 233.

30 Bonaventure, *Itinerarium Mentis in Deum*, 2.

31 On which see R. H. Stephenson, *Goethe's Conception of Knowledge and Science*. Edinburgh: Edinburgh University Press, 1995.

32 *A Devil's Chaplain*, 139.

33 *A Devil's Chaplain*, 19.

34  *A Devil's Chaplain*, 18–19. He cites in support Lewis Wolpert's excellent study, *The Unnatural Nature of Science*. London: Faber & Faber, 1992.

35  Bas van Fraassen, "Empiricism in the Philosophy of Science." In *Images of Science: Essays on Realism and Empiricism*, edited by P. Churchland and C. Hooker, 245–308. Chicago: University of Chicago Press, 1985. Quote at 258.

36  *Unweaving the Rainbow*, 17.

37  Charles Gore, *The Incarnation of the Son of God*. London: John Murray, 1922, 105–6.

38  *Unweaving the Rainbow*, 313.

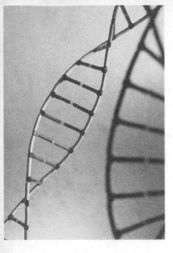

# Works Consulted

Allen, Garland. "T. H. Morgan and the Emergence of a New American Biology." *Quarterly Review of Biology* 44 (1969): 166–88.

Alter, Stephen G. *Darwinism and the Linguistic Image: Language, Race, and Natural Theology in the Nineteenth Century.* Baltimore, MD: Johns Hopkins University Press, 1999.

Aunger, Robert, ed. *Darwinizing Culture: The Status of Memetics as a Science.* Oxford: Oxford University Press, 2000.

Avery, Oswald, Colin MacLeod, and Maclyn McCarty. "Studies on the Chemical Nature of the Substance Inducing Transformation of Pneumococcal Types: Induction of Transformation by a Desoxyribonucleic Acid Fraction Isolated from Pneumococcus Type III." *Journal of Experimental Medicine* 79 (1944): 137–58.

Ayala, Francisco J. "Teleological Explanations vs. Teleology." *History and Philosophy of the Life Sciences* 20 (1998): 41–50.

Badash, Lawrence. "The Completeness of Nineteenth-Century Science." *Isis* 63 (1973): 48–58.

Ball, John A. "Memes as Replicators." *Ethology and Sociology* 5 (1984): 145–61.

Bannister, Robert C. *Social Darwinism: Science and Myth in Anglo-American Social Thought.* Philadelphia, PA: Temple University Press, 1979.

Bateson, William. *Mendel's Principles of Heredity*. Cambridge: Cambridge University Press, 1909.

Beer, Gillian. *Darwin's Plots: Evolutionary Narrative in Darwin, George Eliot, and Nineteenth-Century Fiction*, 2nd edn. Cambridge: Cambridge University Press, 2000.

Benachenhou, L. N., P. Forterre, and B. Labedan. "Evolution of Glutamate Dehydrogenase Genes: Evidence for Two Paralogous Protein Families and Unusual Branching Patterns of the Archaebacteria in the Universal Tree of Life." *Journal of Molecular Evolution* 36 (1993): 335–46.

Benzer, Seymour. "The Elementary Units of Heredity." In *The Chemical Basis of Heredity*, edited by W. D. McElroy and B. Glass, 70–93. Baltimore, MD: Johns Hopkins University Press, 1957.

Berry, R. J. *Neo-Darwinism*. London: Edward Arnold, 1982.

Bikhchandani, S., D. Hirshleifer, and I. Welch. "A Theory of Fads, Fashion, Custom, and Cultural Change as Informational Cascades." *Journal of Political Economy* 100 (1992): 992–1026.

—— "Learning from the Behavior of Others: Conformity, Fads, and Informational Cascades." *Journal of Economic Perspectives* 12 (1998): 151–70.

Blackmore, Susan J. *The Meme Machine*. Oxford: Oxford University Press, 1999.

Bowker, John W. *Is God a Virus?: Genes, Culture and Religion*. London: SPCK, 1995.

Bowler, Peter J. "Darwinism and the Argument from Design: Suggestions for a Reevaluation." *Journal of the History of Biology* 10 (1977): 29–43.

—— *The Eclipse of Darwinism: Anti-Darwinian Evolution Theories in the Decades around 1900*. Baltimore, MD: Johns Hopkins University Press, 1983.

Brockman, John. *The Third Culture: Beyond the Scientific Revolution*. London: Simon & Schuster, 1995.

Brooke, John Hedley. "The Relations Between Darwin's Science and His Religion." In *Darwinism and Divinity*, edited by John Durant, 40–75. Oxford: Blackwell, 1985.

—— "Science and the Fortunes of Natural Theology: Some Historical Perspectives." *Zygon* 24 (1989): 3–22.

Brown, Andrew. *The Darwin Wars: How Stupid Genes Became Selfish Gods*. London: Simon & Schuster, 1999.

Brown, Frank Burch. *The Evolution of Darwin's Religious Views*. Macon, GA: Mercer University Press, 1986.

—— "The Evolution of Darwin's Theism." *Journal of the History of Biology* 19 (1986): 1–45.

Bunge, Mario. "Analogy in Quantum Theory: From Insight to Nonsense." *British Journal for the Philosophy of Science* 18 (1967): 265–86.

Campbell, Donald T. "Blind Variation and Selective Retention in Creative Thought as in Other Knowledge Processes." *Psychological Review* 67 (1960): 380–400.

—— "A General 'Selection Theory' as Implemented in Biological Evolution and in Social Belief-Transmission-with-Modification in Science." *Biology and Philosophy* 3 (1988): 413–63.

Carnell, John F. "Newton of the Grassblade? Darwin and the Problem of Organic Teleology." *Isis* 77 (1986): 405–21.

Castle, W. E. "Mendel's Law of Heredity." *Science* 18 (1903): 396–406.

Cavalli-Sforza, L. L. "Cultural Evolution." *American Zoologist* 26 (1986): 845–55.

Clarke, M. L. *Paley: Evidences for the Man.* London: SPCK, 1974.

Cloak, F. T. "Is a Cultural Ethology Possible?" *Human Ecology* 3 (1975): 161–81.

Cock, A. G. "William Bateson's Rejection and Eventual Acceptance of Chromosome Theory." *Annals of Science* 40 (1983): 19–60.

Coleman, William R. *Biology in the Nineteenth Century: Problems of Form, Function, and Transformation.* Cambridge: Cambridge University Press, 1977.

Collins, Francis S. "Faith and the Human Genome." *Perspectives on Science and Christian Faith* 55 (2003): 142–53.

Conway-Morris, Simon. *Life's Solution: Inevitable Humans in a Lonely Universe.* Cambridge: Cambridge University Press, 2003.

Correns, Carl. "G. Mendels Regel über das Verhalten der Nachkommenschaft der Rassenbastarde." *Berichte der deutschen botanischen Gesellschaft* 18 (1900): 158–68.

Corsi, Pietro. *Science and Religion: Baden Powell and the Anglican Debate.* Cambridge: Cambridge University Press, 1988.

Crick, Francis H. C. and James D. Watson. "Molecular Structure of Nucleic Acids: A Structure for Deoxyribose Nucleic Acid." *Nature* 171 (1953): 737–8.

Culp, Sylvia and Philip Kitcher. "Theory Structure and Theory Change in Contemporary Molecular Biology." *British Journal for the Philosophy of Science* 40 (1989): 459–83.

Cushing, James T. *Quantum Mechanics: Historical Contingency and the Copenhagen Hegemony.* Chicago: University of Chicago Press, 1994.

Cziko, Gary. *Without Miracles: Universal Selection Theory and the Second Darwinian Revolution.* Cambridge, MA: MIT Press, 1995.

Darden, Lindley. "William Bateson and the Promise of Mendelism." *Journal of the History of Biology* 10 (1977): 87–106.

—— *Theory Change in Science: Strategies from Mendelian Genetics.* Oxford: Oxford University Press, 1991.

Davidson, Luke. "Fragilities of Scientism: Richard Dawkins and the Paranoid Idealization of Science." *Science as Culture* 9 (2000): 167–99.

Dawkins, Marian Stamp, Tim Halliday, and Richard Dawkins. *The Tinbergen Legacy.* London: Chapman & Hall, 1991.

Dawkins, Richard. "Selective Pecking in the Domestic Chick." D.Phil. Thesis, Oxford University, 1966.

—— "The Ontogeny of a Pecking Preference in Domestic Chicks." *Zeitschrift für Tierpsychologie* 25 (1968): 170–86.

—— "Replicator Selection and the Extended Phenotype." *Zeitschrift für Tierpsychologie* 47 (1978): 61–76.

—— "In Defence of Selfish Genes." *Philosophy* 56 (1981): 556–73.

—— *The Extended Phenotype: The Gene as the Unit of Selection.* Oxford: Freeman, 1981.

—— "Replicators and Vehicles." In *Current Problems in Sociobiology,* edited by King's College Sociobiology Group, 45–64. Cambridge: Cambridge University Press, 1982.

—— *The Blind Watchmaker: Why the Evidence of Evolution Reveals a Universe Without Design.* New York: W. W. Norton, 1986.

—— *The Selfish Gene,* 2nd edn. Oxford: Oxford University Press, 1989.

—— "A Scientist's Case against God." *Independent,* April 20, 1992.

—— *River out of Eden: A Darwinian View of Life.* London: Phoenix, 1995.

—— *Climbing Mount Improbable.* London: Viking, 1996.

—— "A Survival Machine." In *The Third Culture,* edited by John Brockman, 75–95. New York: Simon & Schuster, 1996.

—— *Unweaving the Rainbow: Science, Delusion and the Appetite for Wonder.* London: Penguin Books, 1998.

—— *A Devil's Chaplain.* London: Weidenfeld & Nicolson, 2003.

Dawkins, Richard and Marian Stamp Dawkins. "Decisions and the Uncertainty of Behaviour." *Behaviour* 45 (1973): 83–103.

Delius, Juan D. "The Nature of Culture." In *The Tinbergen Legacy,* edited by M. S. Dawkins, T. R. Halliday, and R. Dawkins, 75–99. London: Chapman & Hall, 1991.

Dennett, Daniel C. *Darwin's Dangerous Idea: Evolution and the Meaning of Life*. New York: Simon & Schuster, 1995.

Desmond, Adrian and James Moore. *Darwin*. London: Michael Joseph, 1991.

Di Trocchio, F. "Mendel's Experiments: A Reinterpretation." *Journal of the History of Biology* 24 (1991): 485–519.

Durham, William H. *Coevolution: Genes, Culture, and Human Diversity*. Stanford, CA: Stanford University Press, 1991.

Ekman, Paul. "An Argument for Basic Emotions." *Cognition and Emotion* 6 (1992): 169–200.

Eldredge, Niles. *Time Frames: The Rethinking of Darwinian Evolution and the Theory of Punctuated Equilibria*. London: Heinemann, 1986.

—— *Reinventing Darwin: The Great Debate at the High Table of Evolutionary Theory*. New York: John Wiley & Sons, 1995.

Ellegård, Alvar. *Darwin and the General Reader: The Reception of Darwin's Theory of Evolution in the British Periodical Press, 1859–1872*. Chicago: University of Chicago Press, 1990.

England, Richard. "Natural Selection, Teleology, and the Logos: From Darwin to the Oxford Neo-Darwinists, 1859–1909." *Osiris* 16 (2001): 270–87.

Evans, L. T. "Darwin's Use of the Analogy between Artificial and Natural Selection." *Journal of the History of Biology* 17 (1984): 113–40.

Fairbanks, Daniel J. and Bryce Rytting. "Mendelian Controversies: A Botanical and Historical Review." *American Journal of Botany* 88 (2001): 737–52.

Fisher, Ronald A. *The Genetical Theory of Natural Selection*. Oxford: Clarendon Press, 1930.

—— "Has Mendel's Work Been Rediscovered?" *Annals of Science* 1 (1936): 115–37.

—— "The Renaissance of Darwinism." *The Listener* 37 (1947): 1001.

Fleming, Donald. "Charles Darwin, the Anaesthetic Man." *Victorian Studies* 4 (1961): 219–36.

Fraassen, Bas van. "Empiricism in the Philosophy of Science." In *Images of Science: Essays on Realism and Empiricism*, edited by P. Churchland and C. Hooker, 245–308. Chicago: University of Chicago Press, 1985.

Fyfe, Aileen. "The Reception of William Paley's *Natural Theology* in the University of Cambridge." *British Journal for the History of Science* 30 (1997): 321–35.

Gale, Barry G. *Evolution Without Evidence: Charles Darwin and the Origin of Species.* Albuquerque: University of New Mexico Press, 1982.

Gascoigne, John. "From Bentley to the Victorians: The Rise and Fall of British Newtonian Natural Theology." *Science in Context* 2 (1988): 219–56.

Gayon, Jean. *Darwinism's Struggle for Survival: Heredity and the Hypothesis of Natural Selection.* Cambridge: Cambridge University Press, 1998.

Ghiselin, Michael T. *The Triumph of the Darwinian Method.* Chicago: University of Chicago Press, 1984.

—— *Metaphysics and the Origin of Species.* Albany: State University of New York Press, 1997.

Gillespie, Neal C. *Charles Darwin and the Problem of Creation.* Chicago: University of Chicago Press, 1979.

—— "Divine Design and the Industrial Revolution: William Paley's Abortive Reform of Natural Theology." *Isis* 81 (1990): 214–29.

Glick, Thomas F. *The Comparative Reception of Darwinism.* Austin: University of Texas Press, 1972.

Gould, Stephen Jay. "Impeaching a Self-Appointed Judge." *Scientific American* 267, no. 1 (1992): 118–21.

—— *Rocks of Ages: Science and Religion in the Fullness of Life.* London: Jonathan Cape, 2001.

—— *The Structure of Evolutionary Theory.* Cambridge, MA: Belknap, 2002.

Grant, Edward. *The Foundations of Modern Science in the Middle Ages: Their Religious, Institutional and Intellectual Contexts.* Cambridge: Cambridge University Press, 1996.

—— *Planets, Stars and Orbs: The Medieval Cosmos, 1200–1687.* Cambridge: Cambridge University Press, 1996.

Griffiths, Anthony J. F. *An Introduction to Genetic Analysis*, 7th edn. New York: W. H. Freeman, 2000.

—— *Modern Genetic Analysis: Integrating Genes and Genomes*, 2nd edn. New York: W. H. Freeman, 2002.

Gross, Alan G. *The Rhetoric of Science.* Cambridge, MA: Harvard University Press, 1996.

Gross, Paul R. and Norman Levitt. *Higher Superstition: The Academic Left and Its Quarrels with Science.* Baltimore, MD: Johns Hopkins University Press, 1998.

Hamilton, William. "The Genetic Evolution of Social Behaviour." *Journal of Theoretical Biology* 7 (1964): 1–16, 17–52.

Harman, Gilbert. "The Inference to the Best Explanation." *Philosophical Review* 74 (1965): 88–95.

Harms, William. "Cultural Evolution and the Variable Phenotype." *Biology and Philosophy* 11 (1996): 357–75.

Haught, John F. *God after Darwin: A Theology of Evolution.* Boulder, CO: Westview Press, 2000.

Henze, K., C. Schnarrenberger, and W. Martin. "Endosymbiotic Gene Transfer: A Special Case of Horizontal Gene Transfer Germane to Endosymbiosis, the Origins of Organelles and the Origins of Eukaryotes." In *Horizontal Gene Transfer*, edited by M. Syvanen and C. Kado, 343–52. London: Academic Press, 2001.

Himmelfarb, Gertrude. *Darwin and the Darwinian Revolution.* New York: W. W. Norton, 1968.

Hofstadter, Richard. *Social Darwinism in American Thought.* Boston, MA: Beacon Press, 1955.

Hull, David L. *Darwin and His Critics.* Cambridge, MA: Harvard University Press, 1973.

—— *Science as a Process: An Evolutionary Account of the Social and Conceptual Development of Science.* Chicago: University of Chicago Press, 1990.

Huxley, Thomas. H. "An Episcopal Trilogy." In *Science and Christian Tradition: Essays*, 126–59. London: Macmillan, 1894.

Irvine, William. *Apes, Angels and Victorians: A Joint Biography of Darwin and Huxley.* London: Weidenfeld and Nicolson, 1956.

Keltner, Dacher and Jonathan Haidt. "Approaching Awe, a Moral, Spiritual and Aesthetic Emotion." *Cognition and Emotion* 17 (2003): 297–314.

Keynes, Randal. *Annie's Box: Charles Darwin, His Daughter and Human Evolution.* London: Fourth Estate, 2001.

Kitcher, Paul. "Explanatory Unification and the Causal Structure of the World." In *Scientific Explanation*, edited by P. Kitcher and W. Salmon, 410–505. Minneapolis: University of Minnesota Press, 1989.

Kleiner, S. A. "Problem Solving and Discovery in the Growth of Darwin's Theories of Evolution." *Synthese* 62 (1981): 119–62.

—— "The Logic of Discovery and Darwin's Pre-Malthusian Researches." *Biology and Philosophy* 3 (1988): 293–315.

Koenig, Harold G. and Harvey J. Cohen. *The Link Between Religion and Health: Psychoneuroimmunology and the Faith Factor.* Oxford: Oxford University Press, 2002.

Kohn, David. *The Darwinian Heritage.* Princeton, NJ: Princeton University Press, 1985.

—— "Darwin's Ambiguity: The Secularization of Biological Meaning." *British Journal for the History of Science* 22 (1989): 215–39.

Kruuk, Hans. *Niko's Nature: The Life of Niko Tinbergen, and His Science of Animal Behaviour.* Oxford: Oxford University Press, 2003.

Laland, Kevin N. and Gillian R. Brown. *Sense and Nonsense: Evolutionary Perspectives on Human Behaviour.* Oxford: Oxford University Press, 2002.

Lazarus, Richard S. *Emotion and Adaptation.* New York: Oxford University Press, 1991.

LeMahieu, D. L. *The Mind of William Paley: A Philosopher and His Age.* Lincoln: University of Nebraska Press, 1976.

Lindberg, David C. and Ronald L. Numbers. *God and Nature: Historical Essays on the Encounter Between Christianity and Science.* Berkeley: University of California Press, 1986.

Livingstone, David N. "The Idea of Design: The Vicissitudes of a Key Concept in the Princeton Response to Darwin." *Scottish Journal of Theology* 37 (1984): 329–57.

—— "B. B. Warfield, the Theory of Evolution and Early Fundamentalism." *Evangelical Quarterly* 58 (1986): 69–83.

—— *Darwin's Forgotten Defenders: The Encounter Between Evangelical Theology and Evolutionary Thought.* Grand Rapids, MI: Eerdmans, 1987.

—— "Darwinism and Calvinism: The Belfast–Princeton Connection." *Isis* 83 (1992): 408–28.

Livingstone, David N. and Mark A. Noll. "B. B. Warfield (1851–1921): A Biblical Inerrantist as Evolutionist." *Isis* 91 (2000): 283–304.

Lumsden, Charles J. and Edward O. Wilson. *Genes, Mind, and Culture: The Coevolutionary Process.* Cambridge, MA: Harvard University Press, 1981.

Lynch, Aaron. *Thought Contagion: How Belief Spreads through Society.* New York: Basic Books, 1996.

—— "An Introduction to the Evolutionary Epidemiology of Ideas." *Biological Physicist* 3, no. 2 (2003): 7–14.

McGrath, Alister E. *The Intellectual Origins of the European Reformation.* Oxford: Blackwell, 1987.

—— *The Genesis of Doctrine: A Study in the Foundations of Doctrinal Criticism.* Oxford: Blackwell, 1990.

—— *Iustitia Dei: A History of the Christian Doctrine of Justification,* 2nd edn. Cambridge: Cambridge University Press, 1998.

—— *The Twilight of Atheism: The Rise and Fall of Disbelief in the Modern World*. New York: Doubleday, 2004.

McMullin, Ernan. *The Inference That Makes Science*. Milwaukee, WI: Marquette University Press, 1992.

Manier, Edward. *The Young Darwin and His Cultural Circle: A Study of Influences Which Helped Shape the Language and Logic of the First Drafts of the Theory of Natural Selection*. Dordrecht: Reidel, 1978.

Margulis, Lynn. *Origin of Eukaryotic Cells: Evidence and Research Implications for a Theory of the Origin and Evolution of Microbial, Plant, and Animal Cells on the Precambrian Earth*. New Haven, CT: Yale University Press, 1970.

Martin, Brian. "Social Construction of an 'Attack on Science'." *Social Studies of Science* 26 (1996): 161–73.

Maynard Smith, John. *The Theory of Evolution*. Cambridge: Cambridge University Press, 1995.

Mayr, Ernst. "The Multiple Meanings of 'Teleological'." *History and Philosophy of the Life Sciences* 20 (1998): 35–40.

Mendel, Gregor Johann. "Versuche über Pflanzen-Hybriden." *Verhandlungen des naturforschenden Vereins in Brünn* 4 (1866): 3–47.

Midgley, Mary. "Gene-Juggling." *Philosophy* 54 (1979): 439–58.

—— "Selfish Genes and Social Darwinism." *Philosophy* 58 (1983): 365–77.

Miller, Geoffrey. *The Mating Mind: How Sexual Choice Shaped the Evolution of Human Nature*. London: Vintage, 2001.

Miller, W. R. and C. E. Thoreson. "Spirituality, Religion, and Health: An Emerging Research Field." *American Psychologist* 58 (2003): 24–35.

Moffat, James. "Tertullian and Aristotle." *Journal of Theological Studies* 17 (1916): 170–1.

Moore, James R. *The Post-Darwinian Controversies: A Study of the Protestant Struggle to Come to Terms with Darwin in Great Britain and America, 1870–1900*. Cambridge: Cambridge University Press, 1979.

—— "Deconstructing Darwinism: The Politics of Evolution in the 1860s." *Journal of the History of Biology* 24 (1991): 353–408.

—— *The Darwin Legend*. London: Hodder & Stoughton, 1995.

Morgan, Thomas H. *The Theory of the Gene*. New Haven, CT: Yale University Press, 1926.

Morris, Richard. *The Evolutionists: The Struggle for Darwin's Soul*. New York: W. H. Freeman, 2001.

Nisbett, Richard E. and Lee D. Ross. *Human Inference: Strategies and Shortcomings of Social Judgment*. Englewood Cliffs, NJ: Prentice-Hall, 1980.

Orel, Vítezslav. *Gregor Mendel: The First Geneticist*. Oxford: Oxford University Press, 1996.

Ospovat, Dov. *The Development of Darwin's Theory: Natural History, Natural Theology, and Natural Selection, 1838–1859*. Cambridge: Cambridge University Press, 1995.

Pennisi, Elizabeth. "Is It Time to Uproot the Tree of Life?" *Science as Culture* 284 (1999): 1305–7.

Plantinga, Alvin. *Warranted Christian Belief*. Oxford: Oxford University Press, 2000.

Poulshock, Joseph. "Universal Darwinism and the Potential of Memetics." *Quarterly Review of Biology* 77 (2002): 174–5.

Richards, R. J. *Darwin and the Emergence of Evolutionary Theories of Mind and Behaviour*. Chicago: University of Chicago Press, 1987.

Roberts, Jon H. *Darwinism and the Divine in America*. Madison: University of Wisconsin Press, 1988.

Rogers, Everett M. *The Diffusion of Innovations*. New York: Free Press, 1995.

Rose, Steven. "The Rise of Neurogenetic Determinism." In *Consciousness and Human Identity*, edited by John Cornwell, 86–100. Oxford: Oxford University Press, 1998.

Ruse, Michael. "Darwin's Debt to Philosophy: An Examination of the Influence of the Philosophical Ideas of John F. Herschel and William Whewell on the Development of Charles Darwin's Theory of Evolution." *Studies in the History and Philosophy of Science* 66 (1975): 159–81.

—— *Taking Darwin Seriously: A Naturalistic Approach to Philosophy*. New York: Prometheus Books, 1998.

—— *Mystery of Mysteries: Is Evolution a Social Construction?* Cambridge, MA: Harvard University Press, 1999.

—— *Can a Darwinian Be a Christian? The Relationship Between Science and Religion*. Cambridge: Cambridge University Press, 2001.

—— *Darwin and Design: Does Evolution Have a Purpose?* Cambridge, MA: Harvard University Press, 2003.

Sarkar, Sahotra. *The Founders of Evolutionary Genetics: A Centenary Reappraisal*. Dordrecht: Kluwer Academic, 1992.

—— *Genetics and Reductionism*. Cambridge: Cambridge University Press, 1998.

Secord, James A. "Nature's Fancy: Charles Darwin and the Breeding of Pigeons." *Isis* 72 (1981): 163–86.

191

—— *Victorian Sensation: The Extraordinary Publication, Reception, and Secret Authorship of Vestiges of the Natural History of Creation.* Chicago: University of Chicago Press, 2000.

Shanahan, Timothy. "Methodological and Contextual Factors in the Dawkins/Gould Dispute over Evolutionary Progress." *Studies in History and Philosophy of Science* 31 (2001): 127–51.

Shennan, Stephen. *Genes, Memes and Human History: Darwinian Archaeology and Cultural Evolution.* London: Thames & Hudson, 2002.

Sider, Robert D. *Ancient Rhetoric and the Art of Tertullian.* Oxford: Oxford University Press, 1971.

—— "Credo Quia Absurdum?" *Classical World* 73 (1978): 417–19.

Sloan, Phillip R. "Darwin on Nature and Divinity." *Osiris* 16 (2001): 251–69.

Sober, Elliott R. "Modus Darwin." *Biology and Philosophy* 14 (1999): 253–78.

Stamos, David N. "Popper, Falsifiability, and Evolutionary Biology." *Biology and Philosophy* 11 (1996): 161–91.

Sterelny, Kim. *Dawkins vs. Gould: Survival of the Fittest.* Cambridge: Icon Books, 2001.

Sulloway, Frank J. "Darwin and His Finches: The Evolution of a Legend." *Journal of the History of Biology* 15 (1982): 1–53.

—— "Darwin's Conversion: The Beagle Voyage and Its Aftermath." *Journal of the History of Biology* 15 (1982): 325–96.

Swinburne, Richard. *The Coherence of Theism.* Oxford: Clarendon Press, 1977.

—— *The Resurrection of God Incarnate.* Oxford: Clarendon Press, 2003.

Todes, Daniel P. *Darwin Without Malthus: The Struggle for Existence in Russian Evolutionary Thought.* Oxford: Oxford University Press, 1989.

Turner, Frank Miller. "The Victorian Conflict Between Science and Religion: A Professional Dimension." *Isis* 69 (1978): 356–76.

Ward, Keith. *God, Chance and Necessity.* Oxford: One World, 1996.

Watts, D. J. "A Simple Model of Information Cascades on Random Networks." *Proceedings of the National Academy of Sciences* 99 (2002): 5766–71.

Weaver, A. J., L. T. Flannelly, J. Garbarino, C. R. Figley, and K. J. Flannelly. "A Systematic Review of Research on Religion and Spirituality in the *Journal of Traumatic Stress*, 1990–99." *Mental Health, Religion and Culture* 6 (2003): 215–28.

Weikart, Richard. "A Recently Discovered Darwin Letter on Social Darwinism." *Isis* 86 (1995): 609–11.

Weiling, F. "J. G. Mendel hat in der Darstellung seiner Erbsenversuche nicht gelogen." *Biologie in unserer Zeit* 4 (1995): 49–53.

Williams, George C. *Adaptation and Natural Selection: A Critique of Some Current Evolutionary Thought.* Princeton, NJ: Princeton University Press, 1966.

—— "A Package of Information." In *The Third Culture*, edited by John Brockman, 38–50. New York: Simon & Schuster, 1996.

Winter, K. W. de. "Biological and Cultural Evolution: Different Manifestations of the Same Principle. A Systems-Theoretical Approach." *Journal of Human Evolution* 13 (1984): 61–70.

Yeo, Richard R. "Scientific Method and the Rhetoric of Science in Britain, 1830–1917." In *The Politics and Rhetoric of Scientific Method: Historical Studies*, edited by John A. Schuster and Richard R. Yeo, 259–97. Dordrecht: D. Reidel, 1986.

Young, Robert M. "Darwin's Metaphor: Does Nature Select?" *Monist* 55 (1971): 442–503.

—— *Darwin's Metaphor: Nature's Place in Victorian Culture.* Cambridge: Cambridge University Press, 1985.

—— "Darwin's Metaphor and the Philosophy of Science." *Science as Culture* 16 (1993): 375–403.

Zhou, Zhiyan and Shaolin Zheng. "The Missing Link in Ginkgo Evolution." *Nature* 423 (2003): 821–2.

Zirkle, Conway. *The Early History of the Idea of the Inheritance of Acquired Characters and of Pangenesis.* Philadelphia, PA: American Philosophical Society, 1946.

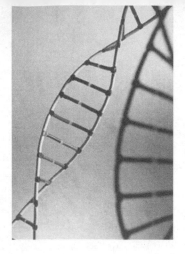

# Index

Feynman, Richard  95
Fieser, Louis and Mary
    114–15, 116
Fisher, Ronald A.  28, 78–9
Fleming, Donald  74
Fraassen, Bas van  155–6
France
  atheism  113
  communism  113
  French Catholic Church  73
Francis of Assisi  153
Franklin, Rosalind  33
Freud, Sigmund  16, 120
fundamentalism  8–9, 78

Galileo controversy  139,
    140–1
Gardner, Martin  134–5
gemmules  25
genetic determinism  46
genetics
  Bateson's theory  40
  chromosomes  30, 31, 35
  and DNA  31–3, 36, 37, 39,
    129
  ethology of the gene  38
  gene, definitions of  38–9
  genome sequencing  40–1
  horizontal gene transfer  41
  Mendelian  25–9, 31, 133
  Morgan's theory  30–1
  mutations  27, 36–7, 39–40,
    44
  particulate inheritance theory
    27
  phenotypic effects  40
  selfish gene hypothesis
    35–6, 41–2, 47, 48
  transmission patterns  25, 30,
    31, 33, 34, 35, 36, 38,
    41, 129
  vertical gene transfer  41

God
  and causality  58–9
  and Darwinism  51, 52, 92
  designer analogy  92–3
  as explanatory hypothesis
    57–60
  God-meme  123–4, 133
  marginalization of  59, 60
  pain and suffering, problem of
    66, 74
  and probability theory  44,
    90, 91, 93, 94
  and the scientific method  9,
    11, 52, 53–4, 55–7
  "virus of the mind" hypothesis
    120, 123, 124, 135–8
  watchmaker analogy  21, 52,
    60, 63, 65
  see also Deism
Gore, Charles  157
Gould, Stephen Jay  10, 53,
    54–5, 80, 95–6
Gray, Asa  80
"The Great Relearning" (Wolfe)
    2
Greek philosophy  15
Griffith, Fred  32
Griffith-Thomas, W. H.  86
Grotius, Hugo  60

Haidt, Jonathan  150
Hamilton, W. D.  19
Heisenberg, Werner  56
Hell  75
Hempel, Carl  94
Hilary, Saint  157
*History of the Conflict Between
    Religion and Science*
    (Draper)  141
*History and Philosophy of
    Science: An Introduction*
    (Hull)  4